What is this thing called leadership?

~ Prominent Australians tell their stories ~

Neil C. Cranston | Lisa Catherine Ehrich

AUSTRALIAN ACADEMIC PRESS
Brisbane

First published in 2007 by
Australian Academic Press
32 Jeays Street
Bowen Hills QLD 4006
Australia

National Library of Australia
Cataloguing -in-Publication data:

What is this thing called leadership? : prominent
        Australians tell their stories.

        Bibliography.
        ISBN 9781875378760.

        1. Leadership - Australia. 2. Executives - Australia -
        Biography. I. Cranston, N. (Neil), 1950- .
        II. Ehrich, Lisa Catherine, 1964- .
        658.4092

Cover and text design by Andrea Rinarelli of Australian Academic Press, Brisbane.
Editing and typesetting by Australian Academic Press, Brisbane.
www.australianacademicpress.com.au

CONTENTS

Dr Neil Cranston is an Associate Professor in the School of Education, The University of Queensland and teaches in the master's and doctoral educational leadership programs. His research interests include leadership and change, aspiring leaders, ethical dilemmas faced by leaders, the dynamics and effectiveness of senior management teams and women in leadership. He is a Fellow of the Australian College of Educators and a Fellow of the Australian Council for Educational Leaders.

Dr Lisa Catherine Ehrich is a Senior Lecturer in the School of Learning and Professional Studies, Faculty of Education, at Queensland University of Technology. She teaches undergraduate, master's and doctoral students and her speciality is in the field of educational leadership and management. Other research interests include mentoring for professionals, phenomenology as a research methodology, and adult learning theory and practice.

Where is the "story" of Australian leadership to be found? What distinguishes "authentic" leadership? And how do people learn about the culture and practice of leadership? Some answers to these good questions lie within this book.

The late historian, Manning Clark, once posed an intriguing dilemma to participants at a seminar on Australian history. If Australia were to have the equivalent of the Lincoln Memorial in Washington, the grand seat from where the carved figure of Abraham Lincoln stares out as inspiration for the passing hordes of tourists, whom we would have seated in ours? There was no chorus of suggestions but the few names that surfaced included Bradman, Monash, Menzies, Phar Lap. Really, was that the best we could do? A very short list including a horse, and a New Zealand-bred horse at that!

Finally, a muted consensus emerged. The great horse was discarded in honour of a man and his donkey. John Simpson Kirkpatrick, that brave soul at Gallipoli, and his trusty donkey could take their place on our most venerated plinth. Regarded as an undisciplined soldier, Simpson risked his life to bring succour to our fallen soldiers on the battlefield before being killed on his twenty-fifth day of active service. However, there was one catch to this choice. Simpson was not actually Australian. The young Englishman had signed up to our merchant marine and, soon after Britain declared war, enlisted in the Australian Medical Corps. No matter. An "honorary" Australian, to be sure, and bound to want to live here had he lived long enough.

This tale says a lot on how Australians feel about leadership. We are very wary about whom we venerate. We are sceptics to the core. We are not easily led. Indeed, Australians rank mateship over leadership. We prefer our leaders to be humble, without rank or rancour or pretension. We are especially reluctant to trust those who actively seek out leadership positions such as politicians.

Surveys consistently rank politicians at the bottom of the ladder on the most trusted professions, below car salesmen, real estate agents, psychics and even journalists! CEOs fare only slightly better. In the 2005 Reader's Digest survey, the Prime Minister ranked 85th and the Opposition Leader 86th most trusted people in a list of 100.

The popular roots of this ambivalence towards leadership presumably date to the convict origins of the nation, the corruption of the Rum Corps, the Irish antagonism to British authority and the ludicrous pretension of the "Bunyip Aristocracy" which generated ridicule rather than respect. In the new upside-down world of antipodean society, class distinctions never got hold the way they had in Britain. We cut down our tall poppies. We don't want people to stand out or get too big for their boots.

Whatever its origins, there is a considerable cultural downside to this antagonism. In sum, it has retarded the development of a mature public debate about where leadership is to be found in this country.

So, where do we go looking to find examples of what might be called "authentic" leadership, the kind that people relate to, respect and can learn from?

Some real-life stories of outstanding leadership can be found in this book. And I am all for getting people to tell their stories because they are an unequalled pathway to learning.

In 2001 I began broadcasting a series for ABC Radio National called "The Wisdom Interviews". These hour-long conversations created the time and space and ambience for a range of distinguished Australians to reflect on their life experiences and distil some of the wisdom that their trials, tribulations and triumphs have brought them.

Then, in 2005, I shifted to ABC Television to present "Talking Heads", a weekly series of half-hour programs in which prominent Australians talk about their lives.

The audience response to both "The Wisdom Interviews" and "Talking Heads" has shown me that Australians really hunger to see and hear our own stories, told in our own "voice". What stood out both on radio and television were the stories of authentic leadership.

The publishing world is drowning in literature on leadership yet nearly all of it suffers from a "translation" problem. It's overwhelmingly about how leadership operates someplace else, in different cultures, with different histories, contexts and values to our own.

Yet, if we are really going to grow in our learning about leadership, then we must know our own stories as well or better than those from elsewhere.

So, that's where this book fits in admirably. It tells the stories of some of Australia's most respected leaders and some lesser-known ones who have also been outstanding in their chosen fields.

They are a judicious choice. Peter Doherty and Fiona Wood come from the frontiers of medical research, a field that has produced some of the greatest ever Australians, including Howard Florey, who developed penicillin. Michael Kirby has built a reputation as one of Australia's foremost legal minds and humanitarian voices. He adds a needed note of caution to the debate, reminding us of the tyranny that many notable "leaders" have wrought.

Four of the leaders have worked through community action. Ian Kiernan has turned the disgust he felt towards the sea being turned into a garbage dump into the international "Clean Up" phenomenon. Although Tim Costello, Jim Soorley and Linda Burney have all sought elected office at some stage on their personal journeys, their work has been very much anchored in their respective local communities. As Tim Costello puts it, "I think people live out of dominant stories and I think my leadership style is trying to tell an alternative story that gives people energy."

Christine Nixon is the contemporary face of the public sector. Through her personal example of leadership, ethics, and energy she has embodied the change that she seeks to make in the role of policing.

Sarino Russo demonstrates that emotional energy and passion are drivers of leadership. As she says, "Your goals get bigger … your commitment is just as strong … So my passion is not going to die". Her story represents the spirit of the enterprise culture which Australia, by necessity in a changing world dominated by globalisation, needed to become.

Maggi Sietsma has poured that same spirit of enterprise and never-say-die attitude into developing the Expressions Dance Company. A fair measure of what makes a country worthwhile lies in the vigour of its artistic culture. And, much of that vigour hinges on the leadership of a relative handful of people. People who are just like Maggi.

Together, these ten stories demonstrate what authentic leadership is all about. Each person embodies their message. Each person amply demonstrates their achievement in what, I believe, are the three tiers of leadership. Leadership begins with an act of creation, a belief. This leads to the need to articulate a set of inner or core "values" that will inspire effort by the individual and the team. Leadership requires constant acts of commitment. The source of commitment is our emotional energy. Without sustained emotional effort our commitment to the belief that propelled us to reach for a vision or goal will dry up. Leadership is also driven by strategy and systems. Strategy is about charting the road to achieve the ultimate goal and the systems provide the means to get you there.

Neil Cranston and Lisa Ehrich have brought together ten stories of authentic leadership from which we can all learn and be inspired.

Peter Thompson
Presenter, ABC TV's "Talking Heads"
Director, Centre for Leadership
Adjunct Professor at Macquarie University's
Department of International Communication
Fellow of the Australian and New Zealand School of Government

Introduction

Leadership — We have all been part of it in some way. Many have practised it, others have researched and written about it. All of us have seen it at some time — or at least believe we have seen "this thing called leadership". It might have been the actions of one of our politicians or business chief executives or sporting heroes or community figures. Or we might have seen it in one of our children as they organised their friends to play a game. Despite its ubiquity, there is a continuing demand for better leadership, be it in business, schools, churches, the community or politics.

The number of books about leadership is as large and varied as the definitions of what writers believe leadership is. A Google search of the term "leadership" generates almost a billion hits! And the supply of such writings about leadership seems unlikely to abate in the future. So, why another book about the topic? And why the title: *What is this thing called leadership?*

We have been researching, teaching and writing about leadership for well over a decade now, and it continues to fascinate us. Part of this fascination derives from the continuing debates about an agreed definition of leadership and another part from the clear significance of the leadership phenomenon and its impact on organisations, the people in those organisations and the outcomes achieved. We have approached this book with different mindsets from our past forays into the field. Rather than take a traditional theoretical approach, we have let the voices of those acknowledged as leaders do the talking. After all, it is such people who actually do it. These are people who live, breathe and practise leadership: they make it happen!

The stories about leadership in this book are from ten individuals. Each has demonstrated outstanding success in their fields, such that their leadership stories are rich and informative, adding both critical and creative insights for those who seek to understand the leadership phenomenon better. There is no doubt that each story answers the question we posed in the title of the book in vivid ways. Not surprisingly, what emerges is a challenging set of vignettes that may provide readers with ways to examine their own leadership style and, potentially, with practical ideas as to how it might be further developed.

It was our intention to present a book on leadership without a heavy overlay of theory. However, our professional backgrounds and the likely expectations of some of our readers did not allow us to achieve that perhaps unrealistic goal. For those who like a little theory — but not too much — the first chapter offers a brief discussion of some of the leadership theories that have attracted interest over the years. It is a chapter that can be skipped by those more interested in reading the words and ideas of our ten leaders. The chapter also introduces one well-known leadership framework as a useful way of drawing out some of the key messages evident in each story. The Leadership Challenge Framework developed by Jim Kouzes and Barry Posner (1995, 2003), used for over two decades in a variety of ways in many organisations, provides a powerful tool to highlight the many similarities and some interesting differences between our ten individuals who answer the question: What is this thing called leadership? We conclude the book with a summary chapter that endeavours to distil some of the pertinent leadership themes evident in the ten vignettes.

We think that the answers our ten leaders provide to our question will interest those currently holding leadership positions in their organisations, those aspiring to such positions, as well as those studying leadership more formally, such as MBA students. We are sure your understandings about leadership will be enriched by the stories of these ten leaders. From our perspective, we feel privileged to have had the opportunity to listen to the stories of these outstanding Australians, and learn more about this thing called leadership.

CHAPTER 1

Setting the scene

As we noted in the Introduction, it is not our intention in this book to provide yet another theoretical account about leadership. Rather, we are keen to let the leaders' own stories evoke both messages and meanings for the reader without detailed theoretical analyses. However, it would be remiss of us not to provide at least an overview of some important leadership theories for those who might find such a discussion valuable in setting the scene for reflecting on the leaders' stories. Later in this chapter, we provide a brief discussion of one particular leadership framework that might be useful to draw out important leadership insights and meanings and we use it to synthesise the leaders' stories in our final chapter.

Leadership has been discussed and debated among practitioners and theorists over hundreds, if not thousands, of years. Quite clearly, it is a highly contested phenomenon that continues to attract great interest and discussion. Indeed, many writers have spent lifetimes endeavouring to identify the specific traits that constitute effective leadership; others have focused on the need to understand leadership in terms of capabilities rather than competencies; and others again make much of the differences between the terms, "leadership" and "management". Regarding the latter point, Blount and Joss (1999, p. 171), two former Chief Executive Officers of large Australian companies, provide an interesting distinction between the work of good managers and good leaders when they say:

> Good managers react positively to change imposed on the organisation from outside … They guide their organisation to respond well to the changes being imposed but give the impression they are being victimised by these changes. But leaders are much different … They pro-actively assess the

> coming changes ... and the opportunities those changes offer to their organisations and they begin to lead their group or organisation in ways to get in front of these changes.

Dubrin and Dalglish (2003, p. 3) argue to be a good leader, one has to make a difference and facilitate change. Some writers view leadership as a process, in which leaders are seen as members of a community of practice (Drath & Palus, 1994). But how did we arrive at such ideas and what are some of the important precursors for these thoughts?

Studies in leadership have examined it from different perspectives, some focusing on traits, others on behaviours, competencies, attitudes and practices. Despite the attention, it remains a somewhat elusive term (Burns, 1978). Over three decades ago, Stogdill (1974) looked at the various leadership theories that had dominated until that time in the twentieth century. Half a decade before, Bernard (1926) looked at traits or the internal qualities one was born with as a way of understanding leadership. The trait approach was very popular for many years and still attracts some attention today, but it fails to account for situational or environmental factors that might be relevant to how leadership is conceived and practised (Stogdill, 1974). Later studies (such as those by Bass, 1981) examined the characteristics and lives of successful leaders, while others (such as Saal and Knight, 1988) looked at the potential of teaching leadership to those aspiring or already in such positions. The work of Fiedler (1967) and others (Hersey, Blanchard & Johnson, 1996, who put forward the situational model) proposed notions of contingency approaches, raising interest in matching a leader with a situation that would be most conducive to that leader's style. The ideas around McGregor's Theory X and Theory Y (originating in 1960) were also of interest around this time (Owens, 2004).

Important leadership thinking has developed from debates about transactional and transformational notions. Discussions surrounding transformational leadership, in particular, are ongoing and there is not the space here to do more than mention them in passing. Transactional leadership derives from traditional views of workers and organisations, and considers the positional power of the leader over followers for task completion (Burns, 1978). Transformational leadership looks at ways leaders help motivate followers by satisfying higher-order needs by more fully engaging them in the process of the work (Bass, 1985). It remains very influential today. Transformational leaders not only cope with change, they initiate it. These leaders personally develop while also helping their followers and organisations to evolve. Underpinning transformational leadership are strong relationships among leaders and others, with the leader providing support and encouragement for individual followers (Horner, 1997). Tracking through the last 100 years, Schein's (1985) work (significant for connecting organisational culture and leadership) is also prominent in leadership studies. More recently, we have seen leadership theories drawing on notions of multiple, distributed or shared leadership (Limerick, Cunnington & Crowther, 2002), moral and ethical leadership (Shapiro & Stefkovich, 2001), critical leadership and management (Fournier & Grey, 2000), and emotional intelligence (Goleman, 2005).

Of course, in our deliberations of leadership we need to be acutely aware of the rapidly changing and unpredictable world and local environment in which leadership is enacted. That is, leadership is practised in dynamic contexts. Some draw on the notion of discontinuous change (Limerick, Cunnington & Crowther, 2002) to capture the idea that the past does not or cannot prepare us for the future. Who, for example, could have accurately predicted the political, social and economic impacts of terrorism on the world today and the subsequent implications for leaders everywhere, whether one focuses on political, business, community or educational contexts? Leadership, then, does not exist within a political, social, economic or time vacuum; leaders are born at a particular time in history into a particular society or community (Leavy, 2003; Gronn, 1999). Leaders are products of their environment and their era, shaped by it and as agents, shapers of it.

What all this adds up to is a great deal of writing and promulgation of ideas about leadership. Dubrin and Dalglish (2003) noted a few years ago that some 35 000 articles and books had been written about leadership. However, while there have been many theories of leadership, there has not been a great deal of investigation into what constitutes leadership from the experiences of Australian leaders across a spectrum of endeavours such as politics, the arts, law, business, community, science and other fields. While there have been many individual biographies of famous leaders, there have not been many studies that have concentrated on leaders' experiences of leadership. One exception was a study by Jackson and Parry (2001) that investigated the leadership and management philosophies of Chief

Executive Officers in New Zealand. Their book comprised interviews with nine "hero managers" who led their companies through periods of dramatic change. Another by Knepfer (1990) reported well-known Australian women leaders' views about notions of power.

The stories in this volume endeavour to address this dearth through what might be seen as grounded Australian vignettes about leadership. They focus on the experiences and understandings from the perspectives of prominent male and female Australians from a cross-section of contexts and backgrounds. Key questions to be asked here are: What do these outstanding Australians have to contribute to our understanding about leaders and leadership? What can we learn from them? To help us answer these questions, we now turn our attention briefly to the work of Kouzes and Posner (1995, 2003) who provide a useful framework against which to consider our leadership stories. (Readers may wish to bypass the following discussion, and start reading our leaders' stories as their first point of entry. We believe they are sufficiently rich to stand alone as significant contributions to our understandings of leadership.)

What attracts us especially to the Kouzes and Posner approach is that it draws on what might be considered some of the best elements of the myriad of leadership theories to emerge over the past couple of decades. We look at this a little more closely in the final chapter, but for now, a short review may provide a useful primer for some readers as they consider our leaders' stories.

Kouzes and Posner identify five aspects as practices of exemplary leadership in their Leadership Challenge framework. While we do not intend to make judgements as to whether the leadership stories offer evidence of exemplary practice or otherwise, we suggest the five practices provide an appropriate lens to look at each leader's story and consider how those stories enhance our understandings of what leadership is like in the real world. Indeed, we invite the reader to make their own evaluation of each story in terms of its relevance and meaning for them. In reflecting on these stories, we appreciate that we need to take a broader view of leadership than just looking at positional leadership roles in organisations. Not surprisingly, Kouzes and Posner also acknowledge this in their model, through one of the leadership practices, "enable others to act".

Kouzes and Posner began conceptualising their five practices of leadership some two decades ago. While there have been some changes in their thinking across that time in response to the

globalised discontinuously changing world in which we live, they
have retained their five key practices as:

→model the way
→inspire a shared vision
→challenge the process
→enable others to act
→encourage the heart.

Each of these key practices will be briefly discussed. We draw largely
on the authors' own words to do this (Kouzes & Posner, 2003).
Because of space restraints, we acknowledge that we provide only a
very limited discussion of their framework. As such, we urge interested readers to investigate the original works for a fuller treatment.

Model the way

Here, it is argued that leaders know that they must be models of the
behaviour they expect of others if they want to gain commitment and
achieve success. Underpinning this is the necessity for leaders to understand their own values, beliefs and principles, sharing these with others,
and more importantly, living them in practice. In this way, leaders
create standards of excellence and set examples for others.

In summary, this is about the leader:
• clarifying and modelling their personal values, and
• setting the example by aligning actions with shared values.

Inspire a shared vision

In summary, this is about the leader:
• envisioning the future, and
• enlisting others in that future vision, appealing to shared aspirations.

Challenge the process

Leaders seek and accept challenge. They search for opportunities to
change the status quo; they take risks and experiment. This is where
new ideas come from and where mistakes can be made. But mistakes,
Kouzes and Posner argue, are learning opportunities.

In summary, this about the leader:
• seeking innovative ways to change and improve, and
• experimenting and taking risks and learning from mistakes.

Enable others to act

Leaders recognise that achievement of goals requires a team effort. Collaboration and trust are key elements here. Facilitation to allow others to achieve requires empowerment, ownership and responsibility. This depends deeply on the development of relationships.

In summary, this is about the leader:

- fostering collaboration and building trust, and
- empowering and strengthening others.

Encourage the heart

Leaders recognise the achievements and contributions of others. Accomplishments are celebrated, and people are valued and appreciated. People are also encouraged and supported in challenging times.

In summary, this is about the leader:

- appreciating and acknowledging the contributions of others, and
- celebrating successes and creating a spirit of community.

What underpins all these leadership practices is the people-side or relational aspects of leadership. They are also values driven. That is, the importance of relationships and working with, and empowering others are critical ingredients of leadership — it is how people relate to, and work with each other, that provides the focus of many leadership challenges today.

We encourage readers to reflect on the Kouzes and Posner framework as they read the following stories. Our final chapter provides a synthesis of the stories employing their framework. We hope you enjoy the stories of these outstanding Australians as they share their thoughts about leaders and leadership. While leadership remains one of the most written about subjects it remains most elusive. We believe that these ten stories make an important contribution to our understanding of leadership today.

CHAPTER 2

Tim Costello

Snapshot ...

→ Tim Costello studied Law and Education at Monash University

→ 2000 — recipient of the Monash Distinguished Alumni Award and in 2005 he was made Officer of the Order of Australia

→ Currently CEO, World Vision (Australia)

→ One of Australia's leading voices on issues such as urban poverty, homelessness, problem gambling, reconciliation and substance abuse

→ Victorian nomination, Australian of the Year, 2006

Tim is characterised by spirituality, passion, commitment — he is strongly values driven, drawing on his Christian faith, and his beliefs in social justice, humanity and equity to guide his work and shape him as a leader.

Introductory profile

Since 2004, Tim Costello has been Chief Executive Officer of World Vision Australia, Australia's largest overseas aid organisation. He is also a Baptist Minister, practising lawyer, university lecturer, author, social critic, father and husband.

Tim studied law at Monash University, Victoria, between 1973 and 1978 and worked as a solicitor from 1979–1981. He left Australia for Zurich, Switzerland, in 1981 to study theology. At that time he became Pastor of the Luzern Christian Fellowship, the only English-speaking church in Luzern. Returning to Australia, he received his Masters in Theology at the Melbourne College of Divinity and was ordained a Baptist Minister in 1986. He worked as a minister in the St Kilda

Baptist Church and then led the St Kilda Baptist Pastoral Team until 1994. In 1995 he was appointed a Minister of the Collins Street Baptist Church and Executive Director of Urban Seed, a Christian not-for-profit organisation responsible for outreach activities to support the homeless and urban poor. Since 1988, he has lectured part-time in ethics and urban missiology at the Whitley Baptist Seminary in Melbourne. In March 2006 he was awarded an Honorary Doctorate of Sacred Theology by the Melbourne College of Divinity.

During the early 1990s Tim was involved in local politics. First he was a councillor in the St Kilda Council and then he was elected Mayor in 1993. He rose to prominence defending the rights of dis-empowered citizens. His term as Mayor was cut short by six weeks due to local government restructuring that saw all of the 205 municipalities replaced with hand-selected representatives by the then Premier (Costello, 1998).

Tim is a well-recognised and highly respected figure. He has not only raised public consciousness about important social issues such as urban poverty, homelessness, gambling, reconciliation and substance abuse, but also been an active grassroots leader and humanitarian.

In acknowledgement of his contribution to humanitarian causes, Tim was Victorian of the Year in 2004 for public and community service and again in 2006. As CEO of World Vision, Tim was made an Officer of the Order of Australia in 2005 for his contribution to inter-national development and particularly the leadership skills he demon-strated in the Asian tsunami disaster. Apart from the multiple roles Tim plays as a minister, politician, lawyer, and humanitarian, he has written a number of books including, *Tips from a Travelling Soul Searcher* (1999); *Streets of Hope: Finding God in St Kilda* (1998); and *Wanna bet? Winners and Losers in Gambling's Luck Myth*, co-written with Royce Millar (2000) (Costello, 2005).

Tim and Merridie, his wife of 27 years, have three adult children.

Some significant life forces for Tim Costello

Two important life forces have shaped Tim Costello: family and church. Tim, his sister Janet, and brother Peter, were raised in a middle-class family where his curiosity for learning and education was encour-aged. Both parents were teachers, with Tim and his brother attending Carey Grammar, the school at which their father taught. Tim's father didn't complete university study until after the war, which gave him his educational break. When he was only fourteen, Tim's father had to leave school because his family needed his financial support — even though he demonstrated the academic prowess to receive a scholarship to finish secondary school. At university Tim's father completed an arts degree and it was there he met his future wife, Tim's mother. Tim described his parents as people who:

> valued education highly. In some ways our family was an extension of the classroom. The kitchen table was an extension of the desk and they were both very naturally curious people and when we'd go on family holidays in long school breaks we would be grilled from everything on the capitals of Europe to Australian history.

The family also valued their faith and the local church was the pivot of the community and Tim's upbringing. Tim attributed the skills and training developed at church as being very useful for his work in later life as a leader. From an early age, he was:

> taught how to speak in public, how to present an idea, how to analyse a scripture or a text, how a church meeting worked where people moved motions and seconded them and passed resolutions.

It was at school, home and at church that his curiosity for all things was encouraged. He learned how to ask a good question, to pursue that question, to read and debate. He said it was quite normal for the family to spend two to three hours over lunch to discuss what was said in the sermon on a particular day. An influence during his teenage years was the leader of Australia's God Squad, John Smith. In his late teens, Tim became involved in an evangelical group called Open Air Campaigners that was responsible for organising children's camps and conferences. It was his involvement with this group that honed his communication skills with different types of audiences.

A third important life force for Tim was the experience of studying theology in Switzerland in the 1980s. This important time provided a direction for his abilities.

> It gave me a theological and intellectual foundation for skills that were there … In those three and a half – four years out in Switzerland certainly entrenched an understanding that Christian faith at its best [leads] inexorably to human rights, to justice.

A further life force that deepened his commitment to social justice and equity issues and led Tim towards working for the marginalised in society was his experience of travelling to a third world country in 1986. At this time, he travelled to the Philippines as part of a human rights tour comprising religious trade unionists and politicians. The experience of seeing the suffering of people living in abject poverty caused him both shock and anger. It highlighted his belief that there isn't a good reason why you can't ask the naïve question "Why is it this way and does it have to be this way?" A couple of years later, Tim formed the Philippines Christian Solidarity Group to raise funds and support Christians involved in human rights work (Costello, n.d.). In all the distress and challenge Tim has met, from the Philippines through to the Asian tsunami, he remains optimistic for the future:

> ... hope is the great motivator for me. It energises me. (The Weekend Australian, 2005, p. 10)

Tim's vision

Central to Tim's vision of hope for a better, kinder and more just world is his passion for social justice and his unwavering commitment to a life of service and dedication to others. That life of service has manifested itself in a myriad of ways through the various roles he has played.

Tim received much public praise, and was awarded Officer of the Award of Australia for the leadership he demonstrated during the tsunami disaster at the end of 2005. Tim was one of the first officials of a non-government organisation to travel to the devastated areas in South-East Asia. It was his strong moral message of those of us who have so much must not forget those who have been stripped of everything (Costello, 2005) that resonated with many people. At this time, Tim took the opportunity to make a strong public statement about the need for "debt forgiveness, of increasing aid, [and] of making poverty history".

Tim's humanitarian work was evident during the time he was minister at the Collins Street Baptist Church and operating his legal practice. He established a not-for-profit organisation called Urban Seed, which worked with homeless people and those who were drug affected. He has also been prominent in leading the campaign against government-supported gambling in Victoria in the mid 1990s. Poker machines were introduced into Victoria at this time and the government of the day promoted Victoria's "casino culture" (Costello & Millar, 2000, p. x). He became aware of the devastating social and personal impacts of gambling on people in his local community. He heard many stories from people who said they had never had a gambling addiction, never gone to the races, starting to say they'd lost all their savings and they were having fights at home. This situation caused him to ask some key questions:

> How come Australia has 21 per cent of all the world's poker machines when we're 0.02 of the population? So who made those decisions and who actually is losing the most out of pokies and where are they situated and who is becoming rich? They are power questions and spiritual questions that I guess my leadership has been situated against.

His strong anti-gambling stance was the subject of a book co-written with Royce Millar that attempted to place the personal battle of dealing with gambling within a wider cultural and political context. The book exposes the moral bankruptcy of governments that have grown dependent on gambling revenue and therefore on the continuation of problem gambling and gambling addiction (Costello & Royce, 2000). Tim's campaigning helped to ignite a statewide and national public debate about the extent of gambling in the community. He sees it as an ongoing challenge.

Tim's reflections on leadership

The context in which Tim's leadership story is told is multiple and intersecting. He notes, "religion, politics, law, society [are] my context". While describing himself as a natural leader in a church setting because of his youth group work and ongoing pastoral work, he also refers to himself as a leader who is a generalist and "boundary rider" because he has moved in and out of many professional environments and played a number of roles simultaneously. An example of this is, while Tim was a Baptist Minister at a small congregation in St Kilda, he was also practising law. In this dual role he had the opportunity to represent many people who had been evicted due to ever increasing house prices in St Kilda as gentrification set in. From this experience, he reflects that the logical progression for him was to run for local council and change some of the policies that discriminated against low-income earners.

> I got elected (as mayor) on a platform of putting ratepayers' dollars into affordable housing for people who'd been long-term poor in St Kilda, lived there for generations but were being forced out — which was the first council in Australia to put ratepayers' dollars into housing.

As mayor, he defended sex workers, lobbied for decriminalisation of prostitution, and was outspoken in his views about the unjust laws that left such people vulnerable to attack. As a politician who was also a Baptist Minister, these and other ideas created some controversy amongst members of the church community and wider public — "[I] was a bit of a head turner and eye brow raiser." He was able to reconcile these intersecting roles due to his "boundary riding".

> I do not draw hard boundaries between the sacred and the secular … It is this lack of boundaries between bible and newspaper, prayer and politics that continues to define my worldview and undergirds my passion for life.(Costello, 1998, p. ix)

Tim believes a strength he has brought to the roles he has played in his life is the ability to draw from a wide range of contexts to make connections for people. Yet, a challenge he faces as a leader is to make sense of what is happening in society, identifying its anxieties, shifts, issues. When asked to describe his leadership style, Tim comments:

> I think people live out of dominant stories and I think my leadership style is trying to tell an alternative story that gives people energy hopefully to harness their best instincts for justice; their best instincts for a world where if they could dream idealistically and shape it they would say everyone has opportunity and everyone has access and everyone gets afforded justice. So it's an alternative story. In some of my speeches on leadership I just try and unpick the dominant stories: what I call the wealth to happiness story that says the wealthier you are the happier you'll be. Or it might be the power to happiness story: you know, the more powerful I am the happier I'll be.

Tim also sees leadership as appealing to, and drawing on, the personal aspirations of others:

> I think my leadership style is really around saying if people are motivated by a story that illuminates what's their truest and deepest aspirations then that's what a good leader does, unlocking that and setting it free.

Tim referred to himself more as a leader than a manager since he sees his abilities located in the visionary work central to leadership rather than the day-to-day planning and organising that is characteristic of management. He sees that he is not good at micro-management. His acknowledgement of his strengths and commitment to working with people, are illustrated through his reflections on his relationships with staff.

Relationships with staff

Tim believes that, although his staff and colleagues would probably describe him as a big picture person who sets the vision, he needs and relies heavily on people around him who know how to get there.

> I know that I can only do part of what it takes to actually change an issue, form a movement, build an organisation. My part is the visionary part, the inspiring part, the "come on, we can have a go at this" — but I need a team to actually do the real work of seeing it through and harnessing energies and doubling back and picking up people who fell off. I see myself as a team player.

There is little doubt that Tim's strong Christian and humanitarian values drive his energies and the work he does with and for others. When asked to respond to how his staff would view him, he said the following:

> I think they probably would say "he is fairly down to earth. He doesn't look for particular privileges or perks" … I hope they would say "he tries to live out what he says". I think then they would say "and he has the discernment to try and say well what is the setting here that drives the energies. What causes people — us — to live the way we're living, to work for what — for money, for career, for ambition" and tries to tell a story that says — "it's well written". Not many of us get the privilege of working hard not to make somebody else rich but to make the world a better place, so that becomes hopefully our motivation and he genuinely believes that.

Tim's whole life, his passions and his drive are all about making people's lives better. This deep focus on people is fundamental to how he practises leadership.

Learning

Tim is passionate about education, especially about the issues that are the focus of his work and his leadership — social justice and human rights. He is frequently sought out by the media and other bodies to voice his opinion on a range of social issues. It is through these opportunities that Tim has provoked, challenged and encouraged his various audiences to consider new stories and new possibilities.

> People often say to me that I'm a sort of secular preacher, which always shocks me, because I don't think I'm preaching, but the fact they say that … tells me that it's part of me.

> Everything I do is actually saying "How do I move people who are here? I won't get them right to here but I'll get them a few steps down the road." And how do we take particularly a generation — I love doing stuff in schools and speaking to lower schools. I find young people the most receptive because they can smell the bull a mile off and they are still optimistic enough and naïve enough to ask questions that can change the world and to give them encouragement to have a go at it.

Tim's own life has been drenched in learning: through formal processes such as university and theological colleges. He has also been taught by his diverse first-hand practical life experiences that have taken him to many parts of the world.

Ongoing challenges

In many ways, Tim Costello reminds us of some important aspects of the dark side of life and the world.

> I believe that as a Western culture we have consistently chosen prosperity and consumption before community, belonging and friendship. We have largely opted for competition, not cooperation. Fragmentation, not integration, results. The sense of fragmentation features in our transience ... Fragmentation and transience are strong forces driven by a cancerous individualism that translates into a perverse public ethic. (Costello, 1998, p. xii)

Much of Tim's life has been spent confronting social justice inequities and seeking a more caring and humanitarian approach for all people, especially those dis-empowered socially and economically. Yet losing hope, becoming cynical and despairing is not the road that Tim has travelled or plans to travel in the future. The road that lies ahead is one in which he intends to fight pure cynicism by dedicating his work and life to building a renewed vision for community.

> I want to keep hope alive and nurture the belief that we can build a truly civil and just society. (Costello, 1998, p. 234)

Some important leadership learnings

→ Life forces, experiences and opportunities taken contribute to one's leadership development

→ The fundamental driving force for some leaders derives from a strong and unwavering moral purpose, characterised by commitments to social justice, equity and human rights

→ Influencing others, in the quest to effect change for a better future, is a key challenge for leaders

CHAPTER 3

Christine Nixon

Snapshot ...

→ First female Assistant Commissioner of New South Wales Police

→ First female Chief Commissioner of Police in Victoria

→ Chair of the Australian Police Professional Standards Council and Co-Chair of the Australian Institute of Police Management Advisory Bureau

→ Honorary Doctorate of Letters from the University of Wollongong

→ Honorary Doctor of Laws from Monash University

Christine is characterised by high energy, strong personally held values of respect, fairness and acceptance of others, a strong commitment to her goals, and a belief that at the core of leadership are the notions of responsibility and accountability.

Introductory profile

In 2001 Christine Nixon became Victoria's Chief Commissioner of Police. This was the first time in the history of Australia that a woman was appointed to this position within the police force. As Commissioner, she is responsible for 12 800 staff and an annual budget of $1.2 billion operating out of 550 work locations (Saferoads Conference, 2004).

Christine began her career as a 19-year-old constable in 1973, a time when very few women were recruited to the police force and those who were admitted were restricted in the types of work they could do. For over three decades Christine has fought hard for the rights of women and played an instrumental role in breaking down some of the barriers that have limited their career opportunities. She sees that some gains have been made. Despite this, women tend to be under-represented in senior positions within the police service in Australia.

Christine worked her way through the ranks, in a mostly male-dominated culture. Before becoming Chief Commissioner of Police in 2001, she was Assistant Commissioner responsible for Human Relations in the New South Wales Force (Monash Memo, 2003).

She is well known in the police force and wider community for her anti-corruption stance, strong beliefs in valuing all people (including the marginalised), working collaboratively with others in partnerships to create more sustainable and safe communities, and fair and distributed leadership. She recently took a lead role in overseeing the security arrangements for the Commonwealth Games held in Melbourne in 2006.

Christine and her husband, John Becquet, have been together for sixteen years.

Some significant life forces for Christine Nixon

Christine Nixon was born and raised in the Northern Beaches area of Sydney. She and her older and younger brother grew up in a happy and stable family environment within a supportive local community. Her early environment was a "kind of a big community that worked together ... the kids looked after each other". According to Christine, both parents had "very strong values ... my mother was about honesty and about integrity and about a commitment to the community and ... dad was very similar" (Nixon, 2005, p. 3). Christine's father was a well-known and respected police officer, a ballistics expert in the New South Wales force.

Her schooling took place at local government schools. Due to her fairly strong streak of independence, Christine was Vice Captain and exercised leadership in this context. It was at this time that her skills were extended outside of school through involvement with the local church. She attended Sunday school and, as a teenager, ran a youth group for about 120 children over a number of years.

An important time in her life was around the age of nineteen when she decided to follow in her father's footsteps and join the police force. Her father discouraged her initially because of the force's treatment of women police officers and due to the limited career path it offered. However, she managed to convince him it was what she wanted to do and he became an avid supporter and at times without knowing it, in some ways provided a kind of level of protection.

Another key life force was her journey through formal education. Christine noted it was her father who influenced her to take up formal study to broaden her knowledge base and understanding of the wider world. She began by studying at TAFE. This was followed by studying psychology and industrial relations at Sydney University. She chose the area of industrial relations so she could learn the rules and be in a better position to negotiate with the Police Association over industrial issues that she saw as inequitable and discriminatory. Christine did well at university and enjoyed it thoroughly. Next, she undertook a general arts degree in philosophy and politics and completed it part-time over three years. She described the curriculum as fairly radical left-wing politics that taught her a great deal about theories, politics and philosophy (Nixon, 2005).

A pivotal point of her formal learning was winning a Harkness Fellowship to attend Harvard University. She left her position in the New South Wales police force and returned a couple of years later bringing new ideas and new challenges to her work. While at Harvard, she undertook a one-year masters in public administration, and the second year she worked as a research fellow. Regarding this experience, she said it enabled her to see the world a bit differently and provided the nourishment she craved.

> It exposed me [to] the broader world, not only in public policy but more importantly in policing because of the people I met and the way I was able to work, it was just a far broader base to be able to come from.

As well as these formal learning experiences, Christine also recalls supportive mentors from whom she learnt a great deal, such as John Avery, the Police Commissioner in New South Wales, and others she describes as great thinkers and encouragers. These were "people I saw who worked in government or outside who were just great leaders and people I watched, or people I learnt from, or people who helped out when I got myself into problems on occasions". Christine also believes her learning developed in the different positions she held and through chairing various committees, experiences which "teach you how to deal with people; teach you about partnerships you need to work with". She says that when faced with wondering whether she could successfully take on difficult roles, it

> was a matter of looking around at the people who were doing it and going, hey listen, they're not any different, any smarter or brighter than I am. If they can do it, I can do it!

Christine's vision

As a young woman recruit in the New South Wales police force, Christine became interested in the role and place of women in this male-dominated organisation. At the age of twenty-one, some two years after joining, she became a delegate for the women's police branch of the police association. It was this leadership role that enabled her to advocate for the rights of women within the association and then within a broader context. Her lobbying saw a broadening of opportunities for women and improved conditions such as work and maternity leave. Key issues that continue to be important to her are: sexual assault, domestic violence, child protection and youth policy. She is pleased that over the years the police have started to deal with these issues in a more sensitive and effective way.

Working in a number of positions means she has played many roles and one of these has been an advocacy role. She says, "I don't like to see people victimised, I don't like to see people harmed and policing … allows you … to do something about that". An incident for which she received a great deal of publicity was her decision to take part in the Lesbian and Gay Pride March. She commented that she would show her support for

> decent and reasonable people who want to get on with their lives, and they have been treated appallingly previously by the Police, and I'm prepared to do something about it. And if it's a small symbol of marching with them, then that would be a reasonable thing to do. (Nixon, 2003, p. 14)

Christine remembers a friend saying:

> you need to know what you're going to die in the ditch for because sometimes they'll just run you over … so then you get smarter about thinking about what you're going to stand up for and how you can make a difference or a contribution.

In her inaugural speech as Chief Commissioner of the Victorian Police, she said, "we are the people's police. We are here to serve. We serve our communities, we serve our citizens, we serve our residents and we serve our children" (Nixon, 2001). Her vision of serving others, of treating others fairly, with respect and dignity, are paramount to her work as a leader and officer in the police force.

Christine's reflections on leadership

Very much a product of the 1970s women's liberation movement, Christine adopted the idea that "if they [men] can do it ... I can do it". It is this positive and confident attitude that propelled her to not only survive tough times but thrive in a masculine culture. She maintained that these tough times help you to become very clear about your values and what you think is important.

In terms of her work as a leader, she says:

> I think that leader behaviours are listening to people, being clear about what you're trying to do ... Those sorts of things are all part of that process that you ... work your way through and ... contribute to reasonable leadership qualities.

A line Christine cites about leadership is one that goes like this: "leadership is not about privilege, it's not about rank, it's not about popularity but it is about responsibility" (Nixon, 2005). It is this notion of responsibility that she sees as central to the work of leaders and she expects nothing less of her staff. They are accountable for carrying out whatever it is that has been asked of them. Furthermore, she has little tolerance for people who don't achieve, who don't deliver on what you're asking them to do unless there are issues that are explainable.

In developing leadership throughout the organisation, and leading cultural change, Christine notes that:

> You have to make sure you can hold it over time and that's about planting people in the organisation ... and encouraging those who have got those sorts of skills to be able to do that, and continue on with the right ways of treating people and the right ways of working with the community in partnerships and setting goals and achieving things.

Christine credits a number of significant others and significant experiences as shaping her career and assisting her to develop her leadership skills and abilities. Apart from John Avery, who continues to be a great challenger of her ideas, others have included academics whom Christine met through formal study as well as people who work in government and the wider community. Among these prominent people, Christine admired her mother, who at eighty-two "is a fantastic woman. Just got on with things ... and made the most of it and did the best she could." In many ways, Christine seems to embody that same pragmatic and energetic approach of getting on with the job at hand.

Relationships with staff

When asked to describe how her staff would view her, Christine suggests:

> they would see me as sharing, someone who ... ha[s] ... a set of principles, a set of ways of behaving that are quite consistent so people would see me as someone who doesn't yell and scream ... I would listen whatever the issue might be and try and take into account people's opinions and views and value that and then use that to better underpin the decision making that we might be going forward with.

She also described herself as resolute and focused yet approachable and not distant and that her staff would be clear about what she was asking and what the expectations would be of them. Her approachableness is evident by the fact that she receives hundreds of emails from members of the public on a regular basis, which she endeavours to answer herself.

A focus of her work is associated with the strong team she has gathered around her and played a key role in developing. Of this team of twenty-three, Christine says,

> they like each other, they're collegiate, they think about the bigger picture, not just about their own area of responsibility.

She commented that members of the team are not all alike; their differences provide a great strength to the team. She noted the necessity of developing future leaders who are team players. She said,

> You have got to have a belief in, and a respect for, those people you are trying to lead, because if you don't, then they know it. It is a tough argument to try to convince people that they should follow you where you are trying to go if you don't believe in them and you don't have respect for their knowledge and skills. (Nixon, 2002, p. 2)

Learning

Christine's ongoing love of learning is evident. She continues to read a great deal, to teach when she can at the Australian and New Zealand School of Government, to attend formal programs, and to talk to people who are learning.

Just as Christine values her own formal learning experiences, she sees one of her more significant roles as providing a variety of challenging and stimulating learning opportunities for leaders and aspiring leaders within the police force as a means of broadening their knowledge and skills base. In addition to on-the-job experiences and encouraging officers to take up new roles and responsibilities across a variety of contexts, she cites several examples of structured programs that promote and support police officers' leadership development. For example, through the Early Leadership Development Centre (of the Victorian Police Force), both executive development programs and team leadership development programs are available for enhancing leadership within the ranks. As well, staff are encouraged and supported to undertake postgraduate degrees and a range of international exchange experiences are available. Recently the force has devoted considerable resources to sending officers to many countries to learn more about counter-terrorism issues and to bring that knowledge back. An important part of the culture of learning in the Victorian Police Force is fostering research relationships with universities so that research can enrich the practice of policing. There are several Australian Research Council grants on which the Victorian Police Force is working jointly with Australian universities.

Her message of the value and place of education is one that she sends to members of the wider community, not only the police community. For example, she cited a number of empowerment programs for the elderly and others that are provided by the police as a means of educating the wider public. As Christine says, it is through encouraging programs and ways of behaving that actually makes people's lives better. Christine is a sought after speaker at conferences and special events and her message often harks back to the value of education. As she says:

> I spend a lot of time talking to people in the community and young people and particularly women, to say that education is such an important part of the way the world is, and to continue to study. (Nixon, 2003, p. 10)

Ongoing challenges

Christine identified a number of challenges for the Victorian Police Force, and for herself personally as a leader. A key organisational challenge was described as:

> development of people, developing organisation capacities ... You're always looking to see if the organisation is agile enough

> to be able to deal with the challenges that come with incredibly rapid technological change.

A financial challenge that besets many organisations is:

> managing within what is always relatively tight budgets and how do you choose your priorities about where you're going to put your money?

On a more personal level, Christine notes that achieving a balance in her work life and home life is an ongoing quest. While she admits she does not always achieve this balance, she does endeavour to reflect that model within policing for others on her staff. She says her energy and enthusiasm as well as being optimistic sustain her in achieving her goals and keep her motivated. Furthermore, "when you see things happen and you see organisations and individuals achieve them that ... also inspires me to go 'yes' we can do this".

A final dilemma Christine raises and one most, if not all, leaders face is knowing when to let go.

> you do actually need to know that ... it's all pretty temporary; that you have your time, you have the opportunity and then you need to say that you've put things in place and need to be able to move on.

It seems that Christine's time is far from over; there are too many other challenges beckoning.

Outside of the policing context, Christine recalls a conversation she had with an ethicist who raised the important issue of silent leaders. That is, the challenge of encouraging highly successful business leaders to move into broader areas of endeavour and add their voices to a range of social and economic issues. She sees this as grounded in the notion that "we have a broader obligation ... you can actually make a huge difference because you've got a capacity and an opportunity to do it". While Christine continues to make her mark within the police service, it seems likely that when her time comes to an end, she may well pursue other challenges and apply her considerable talents and leadership capacities to different areas of social and public policy.

Some important leadership learnings

→ Leadership must be values driven — we need to know what is driving us, what our values and beliefs are and what the vision and goals are that we are seeking —these ought be about equity and tolerance

→ Leadership is a people and team process, working with and through others to achieve clearly defined ends — the leader needs to demonstrate respect for all team members

→ Leadership is about responsibility and accountability — it ought reflect energy, enthusiasm and optimism

→ Formal and informal learning is critical to leadership development, enhancing leadership capacities from different fields of endeavour and perspectives

CHAPTER 4

Michael Kirby

Snapshot ...

→ Appointed to the High Court in February 1996

→ Previously President of the New South Wales Court of Appeal; Federal Court judge

→ First Chairperson of the Australian Law Reform Commission (1975 to 1984)

→ Companion in the General Division of the Order of Australia

→ NSW Australian of the Year, 2006

Michael is characterised by high intelligence, high energy, dedication, concern, compassion and humour — he is driven by a deep commitment to social justice and humanitarian principles.

Introductory profile

Justice Michael Donald Kirby was appointed to the High Court in February 1996. Prior to that, he was President of the New South Wales Court of Appeal (since 1984). He has held many national and international positions including member of the Board of CSIRO, President of the Court of Appeal of Solomon Islands, United Nations Special Representative in Cambodia and President of the International Commission of Jurists. In 1991 he was appointed a Companion in the General Division of the Order of Australia.

Michael Kirby attended Sydney University, where he completed Art, Economics and Law degrees, the latter at a Masters level. He began his law career when admitted to the New South Wales bar in

1967. Some eight years later, he was appointed Deputy President of the Australian Conciliation and Arbitration Commission. At about the same time, he was made the first Chairperson of the Australian Law Reform Commission. In 1983, he became a judge of the Federal Court of Australia, the youngest person to be appointed to Federal judicial office in Australia.

Michael has had close connections with universities, serving as a Fellow of the Senate of Sydney University, Chancellor of Macquarie University and Deputy Chancellor of the University of Newcastle. Several universities have conferred him with honorary doctorates, including Sydney University, the University of Ulster and the National Law School of India. He has been the recipient of a number of distinguished awards, including Honorary Fellow of the Academy of Social Sciences (1996), a Companion of the Order of St Michael and St George (1983), Companion of the Order of Australia (1991), the Australian Human Rights Medal (1991) and New South Wales Australian of the Year, 2006. In 1997, the Bulletin magazine named him as one of Australia's ten most creative minds.

Michael Kirby has a deep interest in social justice and human rights issues and has served as a member of the World Health Organization's Global Commission on AIDS. He has also advised UNAIDS Geneva on human rights aspects of the AIDS epidemic.

Despite such a distinguished legal and professional career, Michael retains a remarkably modest perspective about his work and achievements, among both the legal fraternity and the general public.

> I think most of them [the community]) don't really know all that much about what I do as a Judge, because that really isn't known by many citizens ... Lots of long suffering [legal] audiences all over the country have had to put up with me expounding my views over more than 30 years. So I think that is why you get some degree of name recognition.

He takes a somewhat self-deprecatory view to his being appointed as a judge, although it is one that is based on how these events occur:

> I think it is often said that judicial appointment is like a very delicate gavotte which is played with people dancing around the chairs. Then suddenly the music stops and it is a question of who happens to be closest to the chairs.

Some significant life forces for Michael Kirby

Michael Kirby was born and educated in Sydney. His ancestors on both sides of the family came from Ireland, his mother's family from Ulster and his father's from Limerick (Kirby, 1998a). Michael's parents were religious people who raised him in the Anglican tradition of the Christian faith (Kirby, 1998b, p. 5). While attending Fort Street High School, he was confirmed in St Andrew's Anglican Church and sang in its Church Choir. In an address to the Prayer Society, Church of St Mary the Virgin, Michael reflected on the prominent place the *Book of Common Prayer* has in his life. As a book of services and prayers used in the Anglican Church, he says it continues to inspire him, not only for its beautiful language but also the comfort it provides; it has been a true companion throughout his life (Kirby, 1998b).

While religion has been an important life force for Michael, he has been a vocal critic of the church for its mistreatment of certain groups in society such as women, drug dependent people and homosexuals (Kirby, 2000). Yet, for other groups, such as the poor, sick and unemployed, Michael has observed that the churches have shown compassion and have displayed an admirable record of defending human rights (Kirby, 2000).

Another important life force for Michael was his time at school that laid the foundations for him to expand his mind and sharpen his skills in expressing himself and convincing others of his ideas and opinions. He was an outstanding student who participated in debating, public speaking and acting in plays. He had a particular interest in, and academic capacity for, history — he came first in NSW's leaving exams in the subject of modern history. This interest in, and appreciation for, history has a major influence on his views about leadership, particularly leadership enacted in political contexts. Thinking back on his career, Michael suggests that he "should have been a historian, not a lawyer. In fact, I feel very frustrated that I took that wrong turning in my life."

Compared with other legal people and their careers, Michael acknowledges that some of his achievements have come about in a different way.

> I expect that I was appointed [to the High Court] ... because I had a long track record as Chairman of the Law Reform Commission ... I then demonstrated ... that I had

concerns about the application of the law to ordinary people. Those considerations and my public involvement in Universities and the like brought me to the notice of the government. They probably led to my appointment, as well as my long judicial service ... I had a slightly different career path because of my early engagement, for a decade, in the work of the Law Reform Commission.

Michael Kirby's rich and varied professional experiences include working in many countries and in many different roles under the broad umbrella of the law. There can be little doubt that these diverse, and sometimes challenging, experiences have had an important impact on him. He is able to reflect on some remarkable events in world history with a close connection to key players in these events. For example, reflecting on a recent visit to South Africa, he notes the leadership contribution of Nelson Mandela to his country:

> It is unthinkable what might have happened in South Africa if Nelson Mandela had not been there ... [He] is certainly a person who I regard as having rare qualities of leadership. They [Mandela and others] were terribly important ... as virtually everyone acknowledges, for the transition to their present Constitution.

In contrast to this positive example of the work of a notable world figure, Michael takes a highly sceptical view of many engaged in the political world. Drawing again on his historical interests, he notes that we all ought to take a keen interest in political leadership as it is most important.

> ... because it has the greatest influence on human rights and on the economy and the lives of ordinary citizens ... [and] the history of the last century, really, was a history that should warn all democrats of the need to be very careful of putting too much trust in leaders ... if we don't learn the lessons of the last century, we will just continue to make the same mistakes.

Michael's vision

Michael Kirby's commitment to social justice and human rights is reflected in his nomination of some of the most significant leadership challenges facing Australia. He identifies reconciliation with the

Indigenous people of our nation, working towards the ideal of a multicultural Australia, and the assurance of equal justice under the law for all people in our country. In all of these, he is arguing for a better world.

> I have learned that there are wonderful people and civic organisations throughout Australia keen to play a part in a wider world. Mobilising the decent feelings of fellow Australians and working, in proper ways, for a better and kinder society — one of true equal opportunity — is often frustrating ... But most people are good. Most are decent and kind. (Kirby, 2001)

Michael Kirby locates his own sphere of influence, the law, as having a critical role to play in dealing with the challenges resulting from some of the worrying political trends in Australia. His comments capture, quite powerfully, his humanitarian-laden vision for Australia.

> It makes the courts, in my humble opinion, all the more important as guardians of the weak, the vulnerable, the poor, the unintelligent, the unpopular, the down and outs, the dissidents. My concept of democracy is a pluralistic one: a communitarian one in which there is space for everybody, within lawful limits ... it is not a new notion. In fact it used to be the old orthodoxy ... True democracies find a place for all people. That is what we need to rebuild our political institutions ... I think it has gone too far and should be reversed. A true democracy is one that respects the rights of the majority, but within the paradigm that protects the rights and dignity of minorities.

In achieving such goals, Michael believes that if someone has something to give that is different and useful and forward looking, then it will emerge. It can happen at every level. In part, this view highlights his scepticism about leadership, and certainly his criticism of top-down leadership.

Michael's reflections on leadership

Michael Kirby challenges those with an interest in leadership to consider carefully the rationale for pursuing it too far.

> ... leader figures have caused a great deal of trouble in the world and in history. We have to be very careful of them. In politics at least, it is basically an anti-democratic notion.

> Leaders are temporary ... They have to be subject to all sorts of check and balances. I am ... extremely sceptical about leadership.

He expands on his suspicion of leaders, especially political leaders, with illustrations from history:

> Fascism, as a political doctrine, was built around the Leader. You saw it in Germany with the Fuhrer. You saw it in Italy with Mussolini ... On the other side of the political spectrum you saw it in Russia with Stalin ... So the history of the last century, really, was a history that should warn all democrats of the need to be very careful about putting too much trust in leaders.

Michael's critique of leadership is not confined to political contexts. He is also critical of some religious leaders who use their roles and position in negative ways:

> ... you can have great religious leaders; you can have mighty Popes and Pontiffs and Archbishops and they can have charismatic power. They can be highly persuasive. They can be leaders. But they can do an awful lot of damage.

However, considering the concept of leadership beyond these contexts, Michael Kirby is more positive:

> You do get people who have a greater capacity to think about the future and to foresee where things are going. So that form of leadership, by example and by writing, by communication, is not as dangerous as political leadership.

Indeed, he does offer some positive comments about those in other fields such as the church, in non-governmental organisations, in business ("to some extent"), in the courts and in the bureaucracy. Good leadership can be found in many different areas.

However, he identifies perhaps reluctantly, three elements above all others that he believes are important to leadership. These are courage, empathy for others, and intelligence and clear sightedness (Kirby, 2001).

These qualities are evident in the individuals he considers to be outstanding leaders, they turn an individual into a man or woman whom others follow. These qualities, underpinned by an assumption that the leader has a conception of where he or she is going, are:

- the involvement of others
- the courage to do unpopular things
- the capacity to communicate and conceptualise
- acceptance of responsibility and accountability
- knowing when to go. (Kirby, 1994)

He cites Nelson Mandela and Mary Robinson (former President of the Irish Republic and High Commissioner for Human Rights of the United Nations) as two individuals whom he sees as exemplary leaders. When commenting on Mary Robinson's various leadership roles, it is possible to identify some of the positive characteristics he applauds in leaders:

> She was a clear example of uncynical dedication to the defence of human rights everywhere in the world for everybody and not just the politically targeted and popular efforts. She was for the unloved, the oppressed. That is the sort of person that I like and leadership I like.

Michael believes leadership is something one cannot be taught:

> It is something that comes from within a person. Our personalities are so deeply ingrained by the time we get any chance of leadership that it is impossible to pick out three qualities and think that, by concentrating on them, we can turn ourselves into leaders, when we do not have the magic "it". (Kirby, 2001, p. 1)

The qualities or characteristics noted above highlight the concerns Michael Kirby raises about leadership in the political sphere. If these characteristics are indeed absent in our political leaders as his comments imply, then there are serious issues for concern.

> I am just suspicious of leaders, especially political leaders. It is healthy and democratic to be suspicious ... I hope that my scepticism will be a suitable antidote; an antivenene against any excessive enthusiasm about leadership as such. Leadership, at least political leadership, is a magic potion to be taken with care. Its consequences need to be watched. Those who take it need to be sceptical and to change the dosage often, for sometimes in the past it has been a concoction that has proved fatal.

In Michael's view, leadership is only as good as the direction in which we will be taken.

Relationships with others

Some of the key principles underpinning Michael Kirby's views about leadership derive from a deep concern for others, especially those who might be considered disadvantaged, dis-empowered and disaffected. That is, his views about leadership are strongly people focused, certainly in terms of what a leader does and the impact of that leadership. Again drawing from a political context, he notes that leadership can also be a power for a great deal of bad and even a lot of evil, as we saw in the last century.

Discussing his personal interactions with volunteers who work with people with AIDS, Michael notes the group comprises those who are:

> gay and straight, very well educated, the not so well educated, just volunteers, just ordinary citizens ... Various individuals give a kind of leadership to the group. Similar leadership is offered at every level in some society. It is not oppressive. It is goodness by example.

Finally, speaking about his own professional context, Michael maintains that both leadership independence and interdependence are evident:

> amongst judges it is not easy to impose leadership ... Judges are very independent-minded people. The independence of judges includes independence from each other. A good Chief Justice by example, by hard work, by organising facilities and supporting Judges, can get a lot out of them – more out of them.

He indicates that leadership is often shared across Judges and in a collegiate court, leadership does not necessarily reflect formal hierarchy.

Learning

Michael Kirby is adamant that we must learn from history if we are not to make the same mistakes, particularly by abrogating leadership to many in the political sphere. This is exacerbated by the role of the media. It is ever more dominant in forming opinion among the citizenry.

> We see a reduction in the intellectual influence of the media. It now lives by handouts, emailed to them by ministerial officers. We see the effective disappearance of the town meeting, face-to-face contact between politicians and citizens.

> Everything is now controlled and manipulated by electronic and, to a much lesser extent, print media. The interaction of politicians with media really calls the tune on the political issues of the day.

In a warning to the community, he cautions that they just aren't paying attention.

Ongoing challenges

In a final reflection summing up his ideas about leadership, he reminds us that:

> We should, therefore, accept leadership where it is good and kind and sharing and concerned for others who are not necessarily like ourselves, but we should be very suspicious of political, religious and other leadership where it disunites and can lead to hate and discrimination against vulnerable minorities. I am not in favour of the latter type of leadership at all.

Michael Kirby urges that we remain aware of the potential negative side of leadership:

> A list of the top ten business leaders ... a few years back, now looks like a catalogue of fallen heroes. Half the list are bankrupt, in prison or charged before courts ... It is proof that gifts of leadership alone, are not enough. There must be that extra dimension: a commitment to improving ... life, liberty and the pursuit of happiness of ordinary people. (Kirby, 1994, pp. 13–14)

Justice Michael Kirby remains very active professionally, playing lead roles in legal and other spheres. Internationally, in late 2005, he chaired a UNESCO Committee that led to the new Universal Declaration on Bioethics. He also advised UNAIDS on human rights aspects of the HIV epidemic. In Australia, he was recently involved in creating a new museum facility in Canberra, celebrating "Defining Moments in Australian History" (Australian of the Year Awards, 2006). He is someone who will continue to enact the courage, empathy for others and intelligence and clear-sightedness critical to good leadership practice and seek to redress inequities when he meets them.

Some important leadership learnings

→ Leadership, at least in the political arena, must be viewed with considerable scepticism — the lessons of history in this regard are powerful and need to be taken account of

→ Leaders can act with good intentions or with bad/evil intentions — they must not be allowed free rein — in this regard, citizens must retain their own sense of judgment and discernment

→ Positive leadership is underpinned by social justice and humanitarian principles

→ Leaders need to demonstrate courage, an empathy for others, intelligence and clear-sightedness; leadership should be understood as the active involvement of others; the courage to do unpopular things, the capacity to communicate and conceptualise, acceptance of responsibility and accountability, and knowing when to go

CHAPTER 5

Linda Burney

Snapshot ...

→ Member of the Wiradjuri nation and distinguished Aboriginal leader in education, reconciliation and indigenous issues

→ First Aboriginal person to be elected to the NSW Parliament (Canterbury in 2003)

→ Previously Director General for the NSW Department of Aboriginal Affairs

→ Centenary Medal; Honorary Doctorate, Charles Sturt University; Director-General's Award for Excellence in Education

→ Named as one of ten "True Leaders" of Australia by the Australian Financial Review's inaugural *Boss* magazine

Linda is characterised by passion, humility, commitment — she is strongly values driven, drawing on her Aboriginality and powerful beliefs in social justice, equity and humanity.

Introductory profile

In 2003, Linda Jean Burney was the first Aboriginal person to be elected to the New South Wales (NSW) Parliament. She is the Labor Party representative for the culturally diverse electorate of Canterbury, an inner south-western suburb of Sydney. Before entering politics, Linda had a high public profile at national, state and community levels for her work and commitment to Aboriginal education, reconciliation and social justice issues. She was elected President of the NSW Aboriginal Education Consultative Group, a community-based advisory group, and worked with this influential group over a period of ten years. She was instrumental in developing the NSW Aboriginal Education Policy and played a key role in shaping Aboriginal studies programs in schools. She was one of the principal organisers of Corroboree 2000 that led to the Sydney Bridge walk for reconciliation. Over a quarter of a million Australians participated in the walk to show their support for improving relations between Aboriginal and non-Aboriginal people. Before taking up her position in state politics, Linda was Head of the NSW Department of Aboriginal Affairs.

Some of the boards on which Linda has worked include the ATSIC National Social Justice Task Force; the National Council for Aboriginal Reconciliation (and member of the Executive); the Media, Education and Consultative Committee and the Events Sub-Committee which coordinated the 1997 Australian Reconciliation Convention; the Board of SBS; the Anti-discrimination Board; the NSW Board of Vocational Education and Training; the NSW Board of Studies; and the NSW Juvenile Justice Advisory Committee. She was Chair of the NSW State Reconciliation Committee. Linda has represented Australia in international meetings of the United Nations Working Group on Indigenous Populations and participated in World Indigenous People's conferences over a number of years (University of Western Sydney, 2004). She was a Keynote speaker at the 2001 International Montessori Congress in Paris.

For her remarkable contribution to different aspects of public life, Linda has received many awards, among them the Centenary Medal, an honorary doctorate from Charles Sturt University, Lipton's Australian Women's Quality Award, the NSW TAFE Medal and the NSW Department of School Education Director General Award for outstanding service to public schools. She was named one of the ten "true leaders" of Australia by the Australian Financial Review's inaugural *Boss* magazine (University of Western Sydney, 2004).

She is Convenor of the New South Wales National Resource Advisory Council.

Linda Burney is mother of two grown-up children.

Some significant life forces for Linda Burney

Born in 1957 to a non-Aboriginal mother and Aboriginal father, Linda Burney grew up in Whitton, a small Riverina farming community in New South Wales. She was raised by her mother's elderly aunt and uncle (brother and sister) who reared her as their own child. They were born in the late 1890s and had lived through two world wars and the depression, experiences that fashioned their views and values which they transmitted to Linda. Linda credited them with instilling in her old fashioned values of respect for others, honesty, courtesy, decency and tolerance towards others.

As a schoolgirl, Linda read and studied, *To Kill a Mockingbird* by Harper Lee, the Pulitzer-winning book that explored themes of prejudice and injustice. This book had a profound influence on her and reinforced the lesson of standing in the shoes of others in order to understand, empathise and fully appreciate others' lives (Burney, 2003, inaugural speech). Her strong beliefs regarding the necessity to respect others and empathise with their plight is captured in the following quote:

> You may be diametrically opposed to some people's positions and what their party stands for but that does not mean you can be rude and it means that you show respect and conduct yourself in the way you expect to be [treated] ... you treat people with decency and ... what goes around comes around.

Linda grew up with lots of homilies and sayings. Two that have served her well in her work, particularly in Aboriginal Affairs, are "you get more flies with honey than vinegar" and "sometimes you've got to lose a few battles to win the war". In relation to the second expression, Linda said it was important to have the capacity and the patience to be able to understand what the war is and which battles can be lost.

In her inaugural speech for the NSW Legislative Assembly, Linda reflected on the challenges of growing up as an Aboriginal person in the 1960s:

> Growing up as an Aboriginal child looking into the mirror of our country was difficult and alienating. Your reflection in the mirror was at best ugly and distorted, and at worst nonexistent. (Burney, 2003, inaugural speech, p. 4)

She commented that in her youth, racism was never far away and remembered being told that Aboriginal people were the closest example to Stone Age man. Yet her Aboriginality is central to her identity and she is proud to be

> a member of the mighty Wiradjuri Aboriginal nation. Wiradjuri country embraces the Lachlan, Macquarie and Murrumbidgee Rivers. (Burney, 2003, inaugural speech, p. 3)

It was not until Linda was in her mid-twenties that she met her Aboriginal father and extended family of ten brothers and sisters with whom she remains close.

Reflecting on her professional life, Linda believes she has been fortunate to have had many "terrific" opportunities and experiences that pointed her in the direction of public life. A turning point for her was in 1994 when Robert Tickner, the then Federal Minister for Aboriginal Affairs, appointed her to the National Council for Aboriginal Reconciliation. At the time, Linda felt overawed to be included on the Council and to be working beside such respected Aboriginal "giants" as Patrick Dodson (Chair), Lowitja O'Donoghue and Wenten Rubuntja as well as other public figures such as Ray Martin, Cheryl Kernot and Rick Farley (who became Linda's partner). She brought to the Council a strong knowledge of education and training issues for Aboriginal people and an intimate comprehension of curriculum and pedagogy — skills she had developed as a teacher and member of the NSW Aboriginal Education Consultative Group. One outstanding mentor and friend Linda credits with enhancing her knowledge and understanding about so many aspects of life and leadership is Patrick Dodson. The experience of working with Patrick on the National Reconciliation Council was a pivotal one for Linda because it helped challenge her beliefs about what it means to be an Australian and reinforced in her mind that the whole reconciliation process must be a two-way process based on mutuality and respect.

> I didn't and couldn't say that I was an Australian. I didn't feel part of it. I didn't feel that Australia reflected me whatsoever and it was really through the leadership of ... Patrick Dodson ... that led me to understand that me not seeing myself in that way was in part my problem ... I can now truly say ... that I feel absolutely Australian. I actually feel extremely special to be part of the first Australians and I have grown up enormously through that process.

Linda's considerable leadership potential and ability resulted in her appointment to the Executive of the National Council within a short period of time. She went on to play a major role in organising the 1997 convention in Melbourne, which was a landmark gathering in Australia.

Since this time, Linda has been prominent in a wide variety of indigenous and broader social issues. She is a keenly sought after speaker, who brings an informed, insightful and refreshing frankness to significant social and cultural issues facing Australia.

Linda's vision

Linda's underlying philosophy is defined by her fierce commitment to social justice, equity, decency and telling the truth. These are values that underpin her outlook on life and have been the vital source of her passion and vision in her work.

Before becoming a member of parliament, much of Linda's work was connected to education and training. A campaign she was passionate about, which later became a reality, was to develop appropriate and sensitive curriculum that accurately reflected key critical events (for example, the initial "invasion" of the land, the stolen generation, land rights, and so on) in the history of Australia, so all children (not just Aboriginal children) would be informed about the importance of these issues and would be exposed to Aboriginal perspectives about Aboriginal issues. Of her involvement in this work, she said,

> I think we made enormous in-roads into … assisting to shape the way in which schools and educational institutions conduct themselves in terms of … responsibilities of telling the truth … It's about all children and young people … participating in educational institutions in Australia.

The premium Linda puts on education has been evident in her own story. She completed high school successfully and was the first Aboriginal person to graduate from the Mitchell College of Advanced Education (now known as Charles Sturt University) in Bathurst.

> Education is the pillar, the cornerstone of social justice. It is what equals us out … It is education that can bring about equity, equity of outcomes. (Burney, 2003, inaugural speech, p. 3)

Linda's reflections on leadership

Fundamental to Linda's views about leadership are two key attributes: "the capacity to understand and value humbleness" and "loyalty". She believes she has been able to develop a sense of humbleness in her personality due to her upbringing — raised by much older people who had old-fashioned values. Furthermore, her Aboriginality and Aboriginal teachings have taught her the importance of being smart enough to listen and learn. A lesson from her time as a novice teacher was to sit quietly and listen, at least for the first year or two, just observing what was going on before expressing your views and directing others. Although such a message might seem harsh and out of step with current thinking, for Linda the need to be open to, and learn from, others' experiences is integral to fully understanding the dimensions and nuances of any issue.

Linda was involved at an early age in Aboriginal politics. Central to her understanding of leadership is the notion of respect and the need to have earned respect before being afforded the title of leader.

> Leadership has to go with respect and that is something that you have to work on over a very long period of time and from an Aboriginal perspective that's really important and it's a different perspective ... Leadership in the Aboriginal community is very different in the way in which western leadership is ...described ... and, that is, ... you will not be told when you are seen as a leader. You will not be told when you are seen as an elder or a senior person. That comes about through the way in which people respond to you and that comes about by the way in which you've conducted yourself over a long period of time.

Linda believes many Aboriginal and non-Aboriginal women in the community embody leadership in action: the "aunties" who are grandmothers, youth workers, volunteers and teacher aides whose names will never be in the newspaper, who work themselves to death in many cases. These are the women who devote their lives to helping, educating and caring for children and others in the community, yet are never recognised. Linda said that these aunties are not and will never be wealthy, do not aspire to formal leadership positions and the trappings associated with such positions, but continue to give unconditionally because there is a need for care and compassion in our community. Many Aboriginal and non-Aboriginal men and women have influenced her life through their actions.

Challenged to reflect on her personal characteristics as a leader, Linda refers to a description used by a government minister colleague who said that she was generous and gentle but there is a steel under that that becomes clear now and again. In addition to this, she offered the term "pragmatic" to explain her outlook on life. One example to highlight this steel and pragmatism in practice was during the early 1990s when she was involved in developing curriculum for the Year 12 Aboriginal Studies syllabus and electives in Aboriginal issues for students in years 7 to 10 students in New South Wales schools. The issue that caused much debate and discussion was "How do you describe 1788?" There was a perception among some of the players on the committee that "invasion" by the whites was not appropriate, yet from Linda's perspective, "invasion" was the "truthful" interpretation of the event from an Aboriginal perspective and the one she was determined to uphold. As she said, the notion of invasion was going to be there or the curriculum was pointless. After lengthy debate and discussion, a resolution was reached and two perspectives were accepted: first, the perspective as told by a person who was on the shore at the time; and second, the perspective as told by a person who was on the boat in the middle of Botany Bay in 1788. Thus, "invasion" was the word utilised to explain the event from an Aboriginal perspective and the term, "colonisation" (not "settlement") was used to explain the perspective of those who were in the boat.

Linda captures some of the critical essences of her own leadership approach, while offering insights for others.

> I also try and be patient … I just think good manners and intelligence are important. You can't be dumb and do this. But a natural ability, a natural intelligence and leadership are not something that pops in and visits you overnight. Leadership has to go with respect and that is something you have to work on over a long period of time.

Linda sees that leadership is not easy, nor without a cost. She believes there is a high personal cost to pay in being a leader who is consumed by intensive and challenging work.

> Sometimes I look at my 20- and 21-year-old children and just wonder whether I should have been home more, but I wasn't and they understand … There is always that sort of pull of whether or not you give enough to the people you love and the people that love you and I think it's rubbish to say you can find balance. I just think that's nonsense when you're as involved as some of us.

Relationships with staff

Linda's view is one that supports a more distributed or shared notion of leadership. That is, leadership that does not reside within any one individual but is the product of interactions among people — the contributions of a group of people who work together to build or achieve particular ends. She believes:

> If you think that leadership is about you, then you don't understand what leadership is about. Leadership is about the people who have coalesced around you; the people that you coalesce around yourself and you're only a reflection of … your capacity to build people's confidence and build things.

Reflecting on her professional practice and relationships with colleagues both past and present, Linda describes herself as a builder. She gives the example of her role as President of the Aboriginal Education Consultative Group where, over a period of almost a decade, she was able to build and develop a strong partnership between government and Aboriginal people. The result was a substantial advancement for Aboriginal education and training in New South Wales.

Learning

Linda identified many significant people, both Aboriginal and non-Aboriginal, who have played a key role in her life and from whom she has learned a great deal. An openness to learning, observing what is happening around her, and constantly reflecting on her beliefs, experiences and practices, characterises Linda's approach to leadership and learning.

> There have been many occasions … where I've been the only woman in the room and even more occasions where I've been the only woman and the only Aboriginal person in the room and you learn something in those situations.

For Linda, while her formal studies advanced her learning and capacity to contribute to the many roles she has held, she acknowledges a significant contribution from her life experiences. Also, the many influential people (from all strata of society) she has met and worked with in her challenge to promote social justice and humanity for Aboriginal people have furthered her knowledge and effectiveness. She highlights the practical side of her own learning:

> I try and make a habit of taking a lesson from the things that happen to me and things I'm involved with and I don't do it every single time, every single day, but I do it regularly.

Ongoing challenges

In terms of ongoing challenges for Linda, there are many. Some of these challenges have been captured for us:

The young are our future and the older our wisdom. We must find better ways to meet their needs and deal them into the decisions …We have one earth. It is the source of our wealth and our communities. It is a complex task but we must look after it. Unless we manage our natural resources sustainably, we are simply passing on the problems to our children. The issues are enormous and we will work through them with co-operation between government and community. I am determined to make the point that Aboriginal people are part of the everyday life of this State [NSW] and have views just like everyone else. The days of fringe dwelling are over. The imperative of reconciliation is absolutely upon us … The core issue is to work with communities to develop the capacity and to focus on economic development so that Aboriginal people can move away from the vicious cycle of poverty and welfare. This can only happen in partnership. (Burney, 2003, inaugural speech, p. 3)

Finally, Linda believes every Australian needs to seriously consider what sort of country they want — everyone has a responsibility to see that social justice is important.

Some important leadership learnings

→ Learning about leadership and developing as a leader from critical life experiences comes from awareness of one's own identity, personal values, beliefs and passions — leadership is a learning journey

→ Leadership is vision driven — it is purposeful and a moral process

→ Leadership is not a solo activity — it draws on and develops from others — it is enacted with, and through, others

→ Leadership is embedded in notions of humbleness, loyalty, respect, decency — and it often comes at a personal cost

---

CHAPTER 6

Peter Doherty

> **Snapshot ...**
> → Peter Doherty (and Rolf Zinkernagel) were awarded the Nobel Prize in Physiology or Medicine (1996) for the discovery of how the immune system recognises virus-infected cells
> → Laureate Professor at the University of Melbourne
> → Burnet Fellow of the National Health and Medical Research Council
> → Recipient of many awards as well as honorary doctorates from several universities
> → Australian of the Year 1997
>
> *Peter is characterised by passion, commitment, humour, modesty, energy, intelligence — and a social conscience. He is concerned about the future of Australia in a context of questionable leadership practices in some areas and the need to address some of the shortcomings of our education system.*

Introductory profile

Peter Doherty is one of a small number of Australians who has received a Nobel Prize. In 1996, with his colleague, Rolf Zinkernagel, he won the Nobel Prize for Physiology or Medicine for the discovery of how the immune system recognises virus-infected cells. The discovery was made between 1973–1975 when both scientists were working in the John Curtin School of Medical Research at the Australian National University, Canberra.

The research attracted many other prestigious awards for Peter and he received West Germany's Paul Ehrlich Prize (1983), the Albert

Lasker Basic Medical Research Award USA (1995) and the Gairdner International Award for Medical Science, Canada (1986). Peter was named Australian of the Year in 1997 for his consistent record of excellence and outstanding contribution to medical science. Other awards include Companion of the Order of Australia, and honorary doctorates from sixteen universities around the world, including The University of Queensland, Australian National University, Edinburgh, London (Imperial), Berne and Pennsylvania (University of Queensland, 2001).

Peter Doherty graduated with a Bachelor of Veterinary Science and a Master of Veterinary Science from the University of Queensland in 1962 and 1966 respectively, and a PhD from the University of Edinburgh in 1970. He has held academic and research-based appointments in the United Kingdom, United States and Australia. Currently he heads up a research team at the Department of Microbiology and Immunology, University of Melbourne, in addition to continuing his research and laboratory involvement in Tennessee at the St Jude Children's Hospital. Over the last forty years or so of his scientific career, Peter has written thousands of words for scientific journals and forums, as well as articles and commentaries for magazines and newspapers. He released his first book in 2005, titled *The beginner's guide to winning the Nobel Prize: A life in science*.

Some significant life forces for Peter Doherty

> Winning a Nobel wasn't what I set out to do with my life, and as far as I was concerned, it was an extraordinarily improbable outcome. (Doherty, 2005, p. 8)

Peter Doherty was raised in Oxley, a working-class suburb in Brisbane, Queensland, where he was educated at local state schools. He and his younger brother, Ian, were brought up in a traditional extended family of grandparents on his mother's side and a grandmother on his father's side. Peter's paternal grandfather succumbed to the 1919 influenza pandemic and the effect of his death on the family was to cast them into severe financial difficulties. Not surprisingly, Peter's father (Eric) was denied a formal education which was a point of some remorse and sadness. However, it was Eric's desire that Peter and his brother receive a better education than he had been offered. Of his father, Peter said, "with his strong encouragement, the desire to learn and understand became the major focus of my life" (Doherty, 1997). Peter's father Eric trained as a telephone mechanic and then moved into planning telephone services in the old Postmaster General's Department. He died when Peter was twenty-one. Peter's mother was a piano teacher who preferred gardening to teaching. Although Peter declined her piano lessons, she managed to pass her love of music to him.

Unlike many of his contemporaries who left school aged twelve or thirteen (after primary school) to take up employment in local factories and apprenticeships, Peter proceeded to high school where he excelled in the sciences and developed a great love of history and literature. Due to his fair complexion (which is far from ideal for the subtropical climate of Queensland), Peter spent much of his time indoors reading. Favourite authors at this time included Aldous Huxley, Ernest Hemingway and Jean-Paul Sartre. In later years, Thomas Kuhn became a favourite author of Peter's for his work on the history of science. Kuhn argued that groundbreaking research leads to new paradigms that replace old ones. Notably, Nobel Prizewinners are typically people who challenge prevailing views and create new paradigms.

After high school, Peter enrolled in a veterinary science degree at the University of Queensland because he wanted to save the world and was interested in disease. He was inspired also by his cousin, Ralph Doherty, thirteen years' his senior, who graduated from the University of Queensland Medical School. Ralph went on to a successful career as a researcher. After Peter graduated from the university, he worked for the Queensland government as a field veterinarian and researcher of infectious diseases in cattle, pigs, chickens and sheep. He continued his work on infectious diseases for his PhD study which was completed in Edinburgh, Scotland.

After his time in Scotland, Peter, his wife and young family returned to Australia where he took up a position at the John Curtin School of Medical Research at the Australian National University (Canberra). At this time, Peter became very interested in immunology and was introduced to a "dynamic, intellectually driven, basic medical research environment" (Doherty, 2005, p. 7). Rolf Zinkernagel was a colleague of Peter's who was part of this intellectually driven community and it was during 1973–1975 that together they made their discovery for the Nobel Prize (Doherty, 2005). Their work brought them instant fame in immunology circles and even wider acclaim in 1996 when they collected the Nobel Prize.

The years that followed have seen Peter create a successful research and academic profile and work across universities in the United States and Australia. For instance, in 1975 Peter moved to Philadelphia where he continued his research on immunology. Following that was a six-year stay in Australia where he took the position of Head of Department of Experimental Pathology at the John Curtin University, Canberra. In 1988 he returned to the United States, but this time headed for Tennessee where he became Head of Immunology at St Jude Children's Research Hospital, a small well-funded institution with a strong research profile. Peter is now living and working in Australia where he continues to research and write in the field of immunology.

Peter's vision

A central focus of science is the pursuit of discovery and innovation. As a scientist, Peter has devoted his life to asking questions and seeking answers through a rigorous process of scientific, rational enquiry. To Peter:

> the practice of science is still high on the list of what drives me, and I am as excited by intriguing new data as are my young colleagues who do the experiments and generate the results. I remain "hooked" on discovery. (Doherty, 2005, p. 140)

Peter says that he did not set out to make a groundbreaking discovery that would win him the Nobel Prize; it was not even a remote vision. Yet it was something that happened in the course of his experimental work with Rolf Zinkernagal:

> Rolf Zinkernagel and I were young guys, we worked in a small laboratory. We were put in a laboratory together because Rolf sings opera and I was the only guy in the place that had any decent musical appreciation. Science is often like that, it comes from chance encounters between individuals. It comes from skills that one of us has and the other complements. (Doherty in Australian Academy of Science Media Releases, 1996)

This collaborative work saw Rolf play the role of conducting the laboratory studies and Peter took responsibility for the mouse experiments and wrote up the findings.

Peter's more recent work has moved much of his research program to focus on immunity to human viruses. His intention is to devote the rest of his academic research career to developing a better understanding of what is going on during the course of immune responses to both influenza and HIV infections (Doherty, 2005). He recognises that much of the problem regarding AIDS in the developing world is behavioural and can be minimised with more pro-active education campaigns to promote important attitudinal and behavioural change. Nevertheless, his passion and commitment to using scientific research to understand and unravel complex problems continues to be strong driving force.

Peter also demonstrates a deep interest in Australia — where it is located socially and politically now and where it might be headed. While critical of many positions Australian powerbrokers take in areas such as politics and wider public life, he identifies leaders he sees as making a contribution to the country — in universities, in business, in the arts as well as in politics. However, Peter worries about the state of education in Australia, suggesting that many of us are "very narrowly educated, and increasingly narrowly educated … I think it's a big mistake". His education as a scientist and his ongoing research-based work possibly underscore this issue, and make it a source of concern and frustration.

Peter's reflections on leadership

In commenting on leadership within scientific circles, Peter noted that like most scientists he tends to operate in an autonomous and independent way. As he said:

> I've really done my own thing. I've run my own thing. I've never been led very much. I'm not all that leadable I suspect … most scientists are sort of independent contractors in a way, especially in the US where you get your own grants; you get your own salary; you work in an institution and it's like a research hotel structure, so we run our groups but nobody tells us what to do, and that's my life … and I work with people. I don't tell people what to do. I work with them and my lab is always collegial.

Within the actual research teams and units, Peter describes his leadership style as collegial and collaborative. He indicates that working closely with others is vital when undertaking complex scientific research such as viral immunity since it requires teams of people to play particular parts that contribute to the overall investigation (Doherty, 2005). For this reason he believes that positive working relationships among all players in the team based on trust and open communication are essential.

When working with trainees (both postgraduate students and novice scientists), Peter notes that he tends to play different roles depending on the maturity and independence of the trainees. For example:

> My job as a PI (principal investigator) might be to bring the coffee and doughnuts, and to discuss any last-minute changes in the experimental protocol that result from some unforeseen difficulty. (Doherty, 2005, p. 75)

Of concern to Peter are leaders who are "obsessive controlling person[s]" who alienate staff; he views such people as a grave danger in a research environment.

> The thing with self-obsessed, controlling personalities is that it's all about their personal motives and power. This is the worst thing you can get with leadership, where it's all about me; it's not about the job.

Often the only solution to a situation like this is for the leader to go before they create more difficulties.

A key quality Peter believes as critical for effective leadership is the ability to make tough decisions and to be honest and open with staff regarding these:

> You've got to take responsibility and you must be prepared to make the big decisions even if they're unpopular … and you've got to explain them. You have to explain why … I've found with people I've worked with as directors, and things I've done, if the decision is unpopular, if you talk about it with everyone and you say, "Look, this is why I'm making this decision" and discuss it thoroughly and ask, "Can you give me any reasons why I shouldn't make this decision?" and if it's a compelling reason then maybe you rethink, but in the end people in control have to take the decisions and they have to take the responsibility.

Outside the scientific, Peter sees a vacuum in political leadership in Australia — or at least, poor quality political leadership at some levels. One aspect of the leadership required in the political context that is lacking is that of accountability and the acceptance by political leaders that they are responsible for decisions within their portfolio areas:

> I mean here's another thing about leadership too that [politicians] don't do. Harry Truman's sign on his desk that read, "The buck stops here" should be at the front of every political leader's mind.

Relationships with staff

In discussions on working with staff, Peter talked about the importance of open dialogues and conversations, seeking his colleagues' opinions and in turn providing his own, about work-related matters. He would ask:

> "What do you think?" And it goes backwards and forwards. Sometimes they [colleagues] get insights that make me realise that I'm on the wrong track in my thinking. I bring age, experience and cunning. Also, sometimes I can see things more clearly than they do, so that's my leadership.

Peter commented that while principal investigators of research projects operate in different ways, most encourage open discussion since all ideas are up for discussion (Doherty, 2005) and sometimes the newest freshest mind can see important possibilities and opportunities from new perspectives. He says:

> I am delighted when they are able to convince me my idea is wrong. Part of my task as a senior scientist is to help them to emerge as the next generation of innovative thinkers and investigators. They have to grow and to become independent. (Doherty, 2005, p. 83)

Respect for and valuing others, regardless of their formal position in the team, is a key component of Peter's relational leadership style.

> The leadership that works in a research institute is direction by walking about. The best directors are the guys who go and have coffee with the cleaners and the professors. It's about communication and about really valuing everybody at every level in an organisation for what they do. It doesn't matter whether they're people who clean the floors and wash the glassware or the people who run the research programs. If you've got that sort of mutual respect then I think you have true leadership.

Learning

Peter argues that to be successful in science, you require an open mind, and to be prepared to drop one line of inquiry and follow another if it looks interesting. (Doherty in Australian Academy of Science/Science Education, 1996). What is also important is a certain type of curiosity and creative thinking. Not surprisingly, Peter commented that he is fascinated by ideas and likes plays because of the ideas that are raised and explored. In fact, his thirst for knowledge goes well beyond science and he has a probing interest in politics, history and literature. He is also fascinated by human behaviour, what people think and the general sociology of things. He says, "I like talking to all sorts of people. I talk to people a lot just to get an understanding of how people see things." The Nobel Prize and his role as Australian of the Year provided him with many opportunities to rub shoulders with famous and highly acclaimed people as well as people from all walks of life. He used the experience to communicate to the wider public many issues he holds dear to his heart including, for example, global warming, global sustainability, genetically modified food, environmental degradation, and the important role science can and needs to play in helping to inform such concerns. He claimed, however, that using one's public voice should be done judiciously. Diplomacy and persuasion are more likely to be effective than preaching from the high ground (Doherty, 2005). One of the ways Peter has spread this message is through his book, *The beginner's guide to winning the Nobel Prize,* which is an attempt to tell people about how science works, and provide an insight into Peter's strongly held views on many topics.

Reflecting on his wide career, Peter recognised that some of his own learning came from his peers and played a useful role in his achievements.

> Dick Barlow ... taught me pathology ... he also taught me how to write concisely, which was probably the best thing that anybody ever did for me actually ... he taught me to be more precise, concise and I think that was a big plus.

Ongoing challenges

In *The beginner's guide to winning the Nobel Prize*, Peter identifies many challenges besetting the human race and the important role of science to provide solutions:

The task of the scientist through the twenty-first century is to advance discovery, evidence-based enquiry and the technological innovation that contributes to solving problems, alleviating suffering, and generating genuine and sustainable prosperity. (Doherty, 2005, p. 25)

Peter also sees some serious challenges in our political and educational spheres. He suspects that these will remain as challenges unless bold actions are taken to address them. "I think Australia is in for an enormous correction of some sort."

Some important leadership learnings

→ Leadership can be seen, like science, as a journey of discovery, of seeking answers to challenging questions — the discovery is typically a collaborative journey with others

→ Genuine collegiality among, and respect for, all team members are critical in achieving desired goals

→ Accepting responsibility, for both good and not so good outcomes, is a key principle of leadership — leaders must accept responsibility and make unpopular decisions if necessary

CHAPTER 7

Jim Soorley

Snapshot ...

→ Lord Mayor of Brisbane (1991 to 2003) — Australia's largest local government authority

→ Prior to being Lord Mayor, Jim was a Catholic priest, a management consultant, advising a number of prominent businesses in both Australia and the United States

→ Credited with having a major influence on transforming Brisbane — culturally and environmentally

→ Jim stood down from office, he was never beaten at the polls

Jim is characterised by vision, passion, energy, commitment and conviction — all of which are underpinned by a strong social justice orientation.

Introductory profile

The 1991 Brisbane City Council election proved a turning point in the professional and personal life of Jim Soorley. The election, which he won unexpectedly with more than 50 per cent of the vote, saw him defeat a high-profile Liberal Party candidate who had held the position of Lord Mayor of Brisbane for six years. He campaigned to improve the capital city of the Sunshine State by making it a more liveable and vibrant place — he also declared he would cut his salary by $60,000, a decision which went over well with the voters. Brisbane is the largest local authority in Australia, with an annual budget of $1.6 billion, a workforce of 7000, and representing about a million people, making it unique in Australia's system of government. Before the election, Jim had spent seven years of his life as a Catholic priest and, after leaving the Church, as a management consultant in Australia and overseas advising on training and recruitment practices.

Jim Soorley was elected four consecutive terms as mayor, a testament to his popularity and an affirmation of the confidence held by the people of Brisbane in his ability. Jim's success was in large part due to the fact he took the people of Brisbane with him over the 12-year period of the city's reform and growth, an important part of his desire to build a stronger sense of community. His achievements as Lord Mayor included transforming the council into an efficient customer service operation, protecting the environment and celebrating the natural beauty of the area, improving the public transport system, and, helping Brisbane to become a more sophisticated and liveable city.

Prime among Jim's achievements was a raft of community-related initiatives that resulted in strong working partnerships with community groups and organisations, aimed at energising and connecting people to their communities. One way this was achieved was through the upgrading of suburban centres and shopping malls conducted in partnership with local-based communities. He also introduced a range of funding schemes such as cultural development grants, community festival grants, performing arts grants and sports grants to help members of the public to develop a sense of village and community. Community festivals were introduced throughout Brisbane where people came together to celebrate and share living and working within their area.

Another important achievement was transforming the council into an efficient customer-focused body that was there to serve the people of Brisbane — a 24-hour call centre was introduced. Environmental protection was high on the Soorley agenda, exemplified by the cessation of sand dredging in the Brisbane River and the introduction of kerbside recycling. Jim Soorley also protected Brisbane's skyline from overdevelopment, created more parks and bicycle tracks, and improved public transport, introducing the sleek CityCat ferries as an integral part of the river scape and transport system. Many believe that Jim was the key catalyst for changing the face of Brisbane to a cosmopolitan self-assured city, with cafes and on-street dining. He had a particular interest in capitalising on, and promoting the advantages of, the river, facilitating the conversion of run-down unused warehouses along the river into modern apartment blocks and recreational areas.

As Lord Mayor, Jim Soorley was able to put into practice both his strong social justice values and beliefs and his well-honed customer service and organisational development skills.

The business you're in ... is a culmination of your own belief system, your own work history, your own design and organisational sort of perspective.

Some significant life forces for Jim Soorley

Jim Soorley identifies three critical events or life forces that impacted upon his worldview and which have affected his personal and professional achievements. The first of these was a trip to the Philippines in the 1970s where he spent one month living in slums with some of the poorest people on earth. He described this experience as life transforming, not only because it helped him to analyse systems and structures but it also reaffirmed his strong personal value system, steeped in social justice principles.

The second life force draws from his time in the priesthood when he worked closely with individuals, often in challenging counselling contexts. These experiences helped him to realise the importance of understanding where people are coming from, and how they are products of their history, culture and education.

The third important learning identified by Jim was the importance of making hard and tough decisions when necessary, and not taking what are typically less confrontational avenues to avoid such decisions. However, for him, this approach took some time to develop as it seemed to be at odds with his more compassionate side. It was during Jim's work as a management consultant both in Australia and overseas when he realised the bottom-line in business was making profit and making the organisation work. As a leader, sometimes tough decisions had to be made as they impacted on other people's lives. Jim notes that each of these critical events "made me who I am and gave me the insights that I've got".

Jim's vision

Jim refers to the importance of having a vision and working hard with others to see that vision move from being a shared vision to a set of tangible outcomes. He does not see it as listening to polls and telling people what they have told you.

> Leadership ... involves trying to influence other people to have outcomes that you believe are good outcomes ... It's about trying to set an agenda, a strategy and working in partnership with people, communicating, challenging, stimulating and getting desired outcomes.

As Lord Mayor, Jim and his cabinet held public forums/meetings on current issues across different suburbs in Brisbane, to create a sense of vision and dialoguing with local people. Jim recalls that some of these meetings "were pretty brutal and harsh, some of them were fine". However:

> ... it's about fronting up and taking the abuse and giving the other perspective ... and if there's anger and hostility, diffuse it, then hopefully move it a bit.

He concludes that leadership is not easy, but if the issue is important, it requires considerable effort to bring people with you and win the argument or win the concept. Jim believes that reform without engagement will only serve to alienate large sections of the community (Soorley, 2001).

As an example, he identifies his vision of transforming the Brisbane River from being a sewer, dump and sandmine to an unpolluted natural resource that could be enjoyed by the public. To achieve this, there were wars to be waged, many occurred behind closed doors and involved heavy lobbying and confrontation. One major challenge for this vision was with people whose houses were situated on the river and who believed that the river and the space near the river belonged to them. Many were unprepared to remove their tennis courts, swimming pools, fences and other personal property from what was public space. Threats of litigation did not prevent Jim from pursuing the matter and in the end the threats crumbled and the space was given back to the public for their enjoyment and access. Heavy lobbying was also required to cease the sandmining operation from the river. As with the public space issue, the outcome was positive and the battle was won. Other related improvements to the river included engaging with architects and designers to build buildings facing the river and opening up the river through the use of CityCat ferries. These strategies contributed to celebrating the river as a shared asset for the people of Brisbane. The example of the river is one of many that illustrates the way Jim engaged in a whole process of getting people to change their perception. On driving towards this vision, Jim notes:

> if you believe in something and it is important, then you have to use every trick in the book to bring people with you.

Another important vision that was realised early on during his time in office was changing the face of the local council into a customer-focused, efficient and computerised operation. When he came to office, he was dismayed by the lack of a customer-service culture that operated and the laissez-faire work attitudes that seemed to permeate staff practices. He set about applying his experience as a sales person and trainer to transform the old culture into one supportive of customers and strong on deliverable outcomes. One of the outcomes was a call centre. He described himself as "pretty passionate about ... a really tough hard nosed restructure of the council to deliver outcomes". The transition was smooth because he helped lead a change management process whereby technological infrastructure and support for staff underpinned the initiative.

Jim maintains that one of the reasons his political administration was so successful and popular was that he and his staff didn't stop, they just kept going. He notes that in politics and in big business today, the tendency seems to be that often politicians stall important decisions because of looming elections, seeing such scenarios painting a picture of the long-term strategic good being compromised in favour of a short-term manipulative fix. Jim's vision of his team was always a long-term plan for the betterment of Brisbane.

> If people see momentum and see initiative, they will come with you ... so I worked on the principle that I could convince people to come with me.

At an organisational level, Jim sees it as critical that the leader brings a sense of vision and strategy to an organisation.

> ... organisations flounder when they don't know what business they are in ... you've got to define the vision, and lay out the business. So for me, it is important to say "this is the business I'm in, this is what is is about. Here are the strategies and objectives and make it happen".

Jim's reflections on leadership

Jim is a leader who embodies vision, passion, fierce conviction and commitment. In endeavouring to capture what he sees as the essence of "good" leadership, he draws on some of the ideas of Cardinal Hume (from the United Kingdom) who referred to the 3 Cs of leadership as "conviction", "commitment" and "compassion". These three "Cs" have come to embody not only Jim's beliefs about what constitutes the key elements of leadership, but also his practices as they have guided the way he works as a leader:

> [the first C is] ... a sense of *conviction* where you really have got to believe in something, whatever it is and if you don't believe in it, then you cannot lead people.

> The second C is a *commitment*, that is hard work. You have to get up every day and you've got to drive yourself and drive the agenda that you really believe in and

> The third C is *compassion*. [While] you might believe in it, you've got to have a sense of understanding and empathy for those who don't necessarily have your conviction or your commitment at the moment.

Jim graphically illustrates application of the model by using it as a lens to look at some current and past Australian political leaders — some of whom can be considered to perform well in say two out of the three Cs, but fall short on a third. For example, he cites one current prominent political leader who has an incredible sense of commitment and a strong sense of conviction yet he seems devoid of any compassion or empathy for others. He contrasts this with another whom Jim sees having strong compassion, commitment and drive yet towards the end of his political career, lacked the conviction to explain his ideas to ordinary Australians and thus gain support. Jim concludes that all three elements are critical to quality leadership.

In reflecting on his own leadership, Jim notes that:

> In many ways I probably am an enigma. There is one part of me that is social justice driven, compassionate ... And there's another part of me that is ruthless and hard nosed ... So, people really often get confused.

In part, this emphasises his commitment to his vision and the drive to achieving the vision. Sometimes it is necessary to adopt more vigorous approaches to achieving desired outcomes. In saying this, Jim is clear that leadership ought be about the future and be orientated in a positive way.

Leadership is appealing to the light side, the good side, creating a sense of future together.

Some leaders he sees as "massagers of the dark side". However, he views this not as leadership, rather an abdication of leadership. In his view conviction must be a starting point for a leader. This aspect of leadership also draws on notions of ethics in leadership, an aspect Jim sees lacking in a number of fields, especially where there is a conflict of interest.

Relationships with staff

In the context of building a leadership team, Jim provides some critical comments about employing staff who maybe more intelligent and more competent than oneself:

> I have always believed you should recruit people brighter and more intelligent and more competent that yourself. And my office was always a very strong place. The staff were on top of the game and the best around. And they were the people who actually were the leadership team for the city.

He rejects out of hand the idea that employing more intelligent people has the effect of making a leader look inadequate or ill equipped for office. On the contrary, he notes that those staff who were "top of the game" made him look good. He didn't want yes-people around him and deliberately sought out people who would question, challenge and argue with him:

> We [the team] would have raging debates and arguments and discussions in my office. And they'd say, "Listen, you've stuffed up when you said that. You shouldn't have done that and this is the problem." But that was fine, they knew they were there to do that.

For Jim, leadership should enable all members of the team (the leader included) to have the confidence and security to engage honestly and openly with the rest about particular issues and decisions. He maintains that, in a challenging and passionate environment, better decisions and better outcomes are likely to transpire: "if you have got energy and dialogue and argument and debate inside, it translates in a sense to energy and dialogue outside [in the wider community]". This passion and energy were central to the dynamics of the council leadership team and contributed to the rich work context and relationships among staff. In dealing with staff who did not fit into the overall structure of the organisation or couldn't agree with his style of leadership, his message is simple: they have to go. He came to this rather dire conclusion when he was a consultant. He learnt the valuable lesson that keeping staff too long in the hope things might improve seldom worked.

> When relationships are not working, leadership is about moving today ... if people are not working out and not fitting in to your overall structure system and leadership concept — get rid of them.

Learning

Jim is convinced of the importance of engaging in learning activities to help him become a better and more credible leader. Formally, his two university degrees, one in psychology and a Masters in Organisational Design and Systems Development, helped him to understand human behaviour more fully. In particular, the Masters degree was enlightening on the systemic issues that really change and drive people's behaviour and attitude.

Ongoing challenges

Jim's decision to leave the position of Lord Mayor of Brisbane when he was still experiencing high success in that role was atypical of what one might expect from a politician. However, the decision allowed him to depart as a winner, having achieved much of his vision for the city. Jim maintains a voice among Queenslanders through a regular newspaper column — his strong interest in social, political and human issues is evident in his contributions, as are his strong social justice principles.

Currently Jim Soorley is a director for several Australian companies, including the ACT Land Development Agency, The Brooklyn Group, and Wireless Broadband Company. In addition, he works as a consultant advising on strategy, management and political risk.

Some important leadership learnings

→ Leaders must have a vision — they must engage others in that vision to achieve desired outcomes

→ Leadership requires conviction, commitment, compassion — leaders must believe in something, they must work hard, and they must have a sense of understanding and compassion

→ Leaders need to draw on the skills, knowledge and capabilities of others to build a quality leadership team — ego has no place in this, and the best and brightest need to be included

---

CHAPTER 8

Fiona Wood

Photo courtesy of
Royal Perth Hospital

Snapshot ...

→ Western Australia's only female plastic surgeon

→ Head of Royal Perth Hospital's Burns Unit and Director of the Western Australian Burns Service

→ Dealt with a large number of survivors from the Bali bombings, 2002

→ Australian of the Year, 2005

Fiona is characterised by passion, boundless energy, curiosity for learning, commitment, modesty, humour, intelligence — she is a problem solver, taking personal responsibility for achieving goals.

Introductory profile

Fiona Wood is a medical scientist, a plastic surgeon, Director of the Western Australia Burns Service and Clinical Professor with the School of Paediatrics and Child Health at the University of Western Australia. With scientist Marie Stoner, she is co-founder of Clinical Cell Culture Ltd (C3), a publicly listed, tissue engineering company that is recognised internationally for its pioneering work in the treatment of developing skin cultures for burns victims.

Although a well-known and well-respected surgeon in her field for many years, Fiona rose to national prominence in 2002 as the surgeon who led the team at Royal Perth Hospital to attend to severely burned survivors of the Bali bombings. At the Royal Perth Hospital Burns

Unit, the surgical team operated for five days to deal with this incredible challenge. Fiona used the groundbreaking technique of spraying on skin cells (known as Cellspray) cultured from the patients' own skin to complement traditional skin grafts to cover their burns. Unlike previous skin culturing techniques that require up to twenty-one days to produce new skin, the technique perfected by Fiona and Marie Stoner's research some years' earlier took only five days to produce. The urgency of the Bali crisis pushed the technology to new limits (Laurie, 2003) and in 30 minutes a portion of skin was processed in an enzyme solution and sprayed straight on to the patients. The aim of this was to greatly reduce scarring and the number of operations needed. For her exceptional leadership and surgical skills, Fiona was named Australian of the Year in 2005, and West Australian of the Year in 2004 and 2005. Fiona is also a wife and mother of six children.

Some significant life forces for Fiona Wood

Born in 1958 in Yorkshire, England, to a coalminer father and physical education teacher mother, Fiona was the second-youngest child in a family of four children. Her parents believed very strongly in the value of education and sport to transform a person's life and encouraged all of their children to achieve their personal best in both (Leser, 2005). Apart from some early years spent in the state school system, at thirteen, Fiona moved to Ackworth School, a Quaker school, in a local village nearby. Because of her excellent academic abilities, she managed to complete school a year early. Not only did she excel in academic subjects such as science and mathematics (she was Head Girl and Dux of the School), she was also an outstanding sportsperson and Sports Captain. As a sign of her varied interests, she received a gold medal for the Duke of Edinburgh award.

While at school, her initial intention was to study mathematics and physics at Cambridge University. However, on the advice of her brother who was at medical school, she changed her plans and followed him. She studied at St Thomas's Hospital Medical School in London.

As a newly graduated doctor, Fiona became interested in burns when she saw a badly scarred 4-year-old child. She thought then that much more needed to be done to help the child, not only in terms of the child's appearance but also in relation to pain and functionality (Leser, 2005).

It was during her training in general surgery in London in 1985 that she met her future husband, a Western Australian-born surgeon. In 1987 they migrated to Australia with their first two children. In Australia, she continued her training in plastic surgery.

In 1991 she became Director of the Burns Service of Western Australia a move that provided her with extraordinary leadership and learning challenges and opportunities. An important professional and personal turning point in Fiona's career was in 1992 when she treated a young school teacher who had burns caused by a petrol fire to 92 per cent of his body. This was a defining time for Fiona: "I wanted desperately to help this man, but he had almost no skin left to graft" (Wood in Laurie, 2003, p. 21). She worked hard to convince those around her that he could survive this terrible injury. Using a recently invented technique from the United States, skin from his groin was sent to Melbourne and cultured by Joanne Puddy under Professor John Masterton. This grew enough skin to cover his body three times over. After a couple of months when it looked as though the patient was on the road to recovery, he developed a severe and debilitating complication. At this time, she did a lot of soul searching and questioned whether what she had done was personally good enough. A weekend camping trip with her family away from this emotionally stressful situation helped her to realise that "Unless I could believe that my best was good enough, then I was not sustainable in this environment". After the weekend, she returned to work with the full realisation that "we had all done our best and that this was a success not a failure". The patient did survive after spending another seven months in rehabilitation.

Another significant lesson that this experience taught Fiona was the awareness of taking too much of the load herself. She decided that she needed "to strengthen the links in the team [to include] psychology and psychiatry" and other professional fields. As she said, "we strengthened those links at that time and moved forward as a group stronger for it". It was at this time that Fiona realised her future was in the field of tissue engineering research (Laurie, 2003).

Fiona's vision

Fiona acknowledges that the young teacher she helped in 1992–1993, who suffered horrendous burns, was an inspiration to her and propelled her to undertake research to investigate how to grow skin more quickly. Her work with Marie Stoner over the next couple of years led them to the discovery of reducing the time to culture the skin and spraying the cultured skin cells onto the wounded area (Australian Academy of Technological Sciences and Engineering, 2005).

An important vision that came to fruition was setting up a burns treatment research foundation. This was the McComb Foundation, set up in 1998 with Stoner. Later, in 1999, they established their company, Clinical Cell Culture Ltd, to commercialise the intellectual property for spray-on skin cells. Registered on the Stock Exchange in 2002, this company which employs thirty people provides spray-on technology to many countries, including the United Kingdom, Europe and Asia. The company is valued at tens of millions of dollars, profits are channelled back into funding research in the field. The impetus for forming the company was to provide the means for the funding of ongoing and future research.

> You cannot just sit down and ask [governments] for money. It became apparent to us early on that there's only so much money for research for medicine, so you have to think of other ways to sustain that research. (Wood in Laurie, 2003, p. 21)

Fiona admits that learning how to commercialise her discovery was a huge challenge since the business world was an alien environment. It required her to rely heavily on the expertise and advice of others, since she did not have the requisite education and/or knowledge about commercialisation and other issues such as finance, marketing and so on. Having to learn the rules of this new game, while acting as CEO in the company, in addition to balancing her work as a surgeon, created much stress. Yet she never considered walking away from the venture. The experience confirmed that being a CEO was not where she wanted to be and as soon as the company became buoyant she returned to her surgical and education work. As she says, "My skill set is in training and education and really ... is engaging science into daily practice and that's where I want to be." It is this passion, this commitment, this central belief that motivates Fiona and gets her up in the morning.

Not surprisingly, Fiona's work and her family consume much of her interest, time, and energy. She revealed that she had not really thought about what she has achieved, until having been appointed Australian of the Year:

> What's been good for me this year has been ... [the opportunity] ... to reflect because people have asked me lots of questions.

Fiona's reflections on leadership

Thinking about her school days, Fiona notes that she played many roles that point to early leadership behaviour:

> I was a very involved, active, doing kind of kid and turned into an active, involved, doing kind of person … It was just the way I was … I was in that [leadership] role very early on. I was in that role when I'd take my school team down to the athletics pitch to make sure they could change the relay baton, so that we had a chance of winning.

Following widespread interest in her work post-Bali 2002, Fiona was invited by a group to speak on the topic of leadership. This came as a surprise and challenge because she hadn't given the topic much thought, although she had occupied a leadership position by virtue of her training and education quite early in her career. She responded to the invitation by deciding to explore the notion of leadership or "have a crack at it because it was something different … and I could learn something about myself as well as learn … from other people". This openness to learning and problem solving depicts Fiona's outlook on life.

She reflects that what she does in her work is in a sense "intuitive" the dictionary meaning of which is "action without thought", since so much of her practice comes naturally. However, she does qualify this explanation by referring to her style as action based on emotional insight, since she adapts her leadership behaviour to suit the particular situation at hand. For Fiona, leadership

> depend[s] upon the circumstances and the time pressure is a very obvious example. If somebody is in front and they are in dire straits, in urgent need, you take the lead and you deal with it. If somebody is in a situation where you've got a problem to solve, there's no time pressure, then you can facilitate the leadership potential in your juniors around you to see how they step up to the plate and respond and use it as an educational exercise. So it's actually very varied depending upon the situation.

This description is a classic example of "situational leadership", an important leadership theory that maintains there is no one best way to lead — what is likely to be effective will depend on a range of factors such as the nature of the situation, the ability and willingness of the followers, and other considerations. Referring to her work context, Fiona reinforces this approach to leadership:

> What we've got is your skill level, your resources available and the patient needs and it's bringing that triangle together for the outcome … [when leading others] you've got the situation needs, your leadership potential and the resources around you, i.e. the other people that are with you in the team. So it's sort of trying to bring those things together.

When asked to describe leaders she admires, Fiona says:

> I admire people who are positive … who actually engage and will use their energy to engage with others — to communicate, collaborate, share and move forward in the problem-solving scenario.

This description is in stark contrast to those people she is critical of, namely, those who "need to sledge to win". Fiona's description of the characteristics of those leaders she admires very much reflects what others might see in her. That is, someone who is a positive, engaging, energetic leader who uses her skills and resources as well as harnessing the skills and resources of others to problem solve and to strive towards excellence.

Among her personal qualities as a leader is her strong work ethic: "Whatever I do … I work hard at it because that's what I am … whether it's doing the surgery or riding the bike or trying to help the kids" (Wood in Leser, 2005, p. 59). Related to this is her belief about doing better, constant improvement, and never being complacent: "You have to believe your best is good enough but you can always believe you can do better and I guess that is [my] philosophy." This is one of the important messages she shared with many of the school children and others she met in her ambassador work as Australian of the Year.

Fiona also exemplifies commitment and resilience in her personal and professional make-up. As she says, once you start something, regardless of what happens to you, "You cannot walk away … so in anything I have great difficulty letting go until the job is completed."

Relationships with staff

Fiona is frank in recounting that her early training as a surgeon did not provide positive examples of democratic work processes or teamwork among her professional colleagues.

> I had come through a surgical training system that was extraordinarily autocratic … we were taught by intimidation and … we were ritually humiliated and we all thought it was pretty normal … the surgeons were top of the pile and there were no questions asked.

Reflecting on medicine today, Fiona notes a shift away from a punitive model of training and an autocratic approach with the surgeon as all-powerful to one that is "moving towards multidisciplinary teams. Oncology is teamwork; burns is teamwork. A lot of things are teamwork and so I'm in a privileged position as leader."

In her time as a medical practitioner she observes she has seen "very dysfunctional teams, no teams and good teams". Her own philosophy is one of shared leadership and shared respect for others:

> you [have] to really develop and appreciate the people as they take the journey with you as head of a team because without it you can't actually deliver the care … I can't do all the dress-ings. I can't do all the physiotherapy. I can't do all the nutri-tion, the psychology, the psychiatry. Not only is it out of my skill set, it's out of my time frame, and so by the nature of the subject matter … we have to be solid in teams.

Fiona is also quick to acknowledge that she has skill deficits and that often people become aware of this the hard way. In reflecting on the time when she first established her company, she recalls trying to do almost everything, eventually realising the potential of the skills of multidisciplinary teams:

> that was a very challenging time because … I didn't have the background education and knowledge. I didn't know the rules of the game … that was a difficult time because I felt very much that my feet were sliding … So it's learning that and so you learn that other people have got skill sets and you work together.

Described by colleagues and journalists as "Superwoman" for her boundless energy and ability to juggle several large balls at one time, Fiona is quick to point out that she does not expect others to demon-strate the same unwavering energy. As she says, "I never expect anyone in my team or anyone around me to do what I do". She operates at such a fast and furious pace because she says, "I've got the energy to operate on a lot of fronts. And I feel like it's a duty almost to do it" (Wood in Leser, 2005, p. 58).

Learning

As a child, Fiona had an insatiable urge to learn; that urge has not gone away but seems to have intensified over the years. An important mentor from her early days as a surgeon was Harold McComb. Fiona met him when he was in his mid-sixties and was impressed by his ability of always trying to do better and to learn from today's experience to make tomorrow better. She learned a great deal from him. He was a selfless, passionate and innovative teacher who continued to be excited by his work and approached problems in novel ways. She says, "I always hope I can keep that spark burning that long all the way to the finishing line."

Fiona's philosophy of learning, research and life is enquiry driven, where:

> You ask one question in research, you may answer it, but you ought to ask another twelve. You never actually get to this elusive top of the mountain. (Wood in Leser, 2005, p. 59)

Ongoing challenges

A key challenge Fiona has taken up wholeheartedly is educating the community about the importance of science in enhancing our everyday lives. In her work as Australian of the Year she has shared the passion and excitement that science offers to children and adults alike:

> It's something of a mission for me to show that science can make a difference in our everyday lives because I think there is still this idea of scientists locked way in ivory towers. It's been an education and a great opportunity to travel around schools and take science off the stone tablet and bring it into reality. (Wood in Bond, 2005, p. 1)

Another challenge is spreading the word about the need for people in the community to take more responsibility for their own health, wellness and education. An important quest of hers is seeking government support to ensure that at least 50 per cent of the Australian population will be proficient in first aid by 2010. As she argues, these basic skills are absolutely necessary for people in all communities and might well save lives. As a case in point, she referred to the hurricane disaster that hit New Orleans in October, 2005, and commented that the administering of basic first aid may have prevented much suffering and death (Wood in Bond, 2005).

In addition to these challenges, Fiona identifies finding a cure for scarless healing as her "professional holy grail" (Wood, in Leser, 2005, p. 59). Not content to rest on her outstanding achievements to date, Fiona says, spray-on skin is not a great scientific discovery. It's part of a journey. We have got a lot more to learn, a lot more to do. (Wood in Madden, 2005, p. 3)

Some important leadership learnings

→ Leadership is driven by a passion and commitment to make a difference, to do better, to strive for excellence, to answer the difficult questions

→ Typically, leadership is about a team-based approach, where the skill sets of the team are harnessed to solve the problem and meet the challenges at hand

→ Doing the best one can now, and doing better tomorrow are important drivers in leadership

CHAPTER 9

Ian Kiernan

Snapshot ...

→ A passionate yachtsman, representing Australia at the Admiral's, Southern Cross, Dunhill, and Trans Pacific Cup competitions

→ Established Clean Up (Australia) in 1989 — first Clean Up Australia Day took place in 1990, since then millions of Australians have taken part and it is now a global initiative

→ Australian of the Year, 1994

→ Officer of the Order of Australia, 1995, Order of Australia Medal, 1991

→ Named a "National Living Treasure" in 1997/98

Ian is characterised by passion, commitment and drive. He has a powerful capacity to engage others — the general public, politicians and business — in his vision for the environment.

Introductory profile

Ian Kiernan is the founder and Chairperson of Clean Up Australia. This is a grassroots community-based not-for-profit organisation whose major goal is to clean and fix up the environment. Ian describes it as a simple and good idea — the Clean Up Australia movement is based on the principle that people do care about the environment and when given the opportunity to participate in a practical way are keen, committed and happy to do what is necessary. Starting small in 1989, the first clean up event was organised for Sydney Harbour. An astounding 40,000 volunteers participated by removing all types of rubbish littering the natural environment. Based on the overwhelming public support for the Sydney experience, the following year saw the campaign go Australia-wide and the Clean Up Australia Day event was born. More than 300,000 Australians volunteered in the first year. Since then, it is estimated that almost 10 million Australians have been involved in Clean Up Australia Days, and other organised clean up days including Friday Schools Clean Up days and Business Clean Ups (Clean Up Australia, website).

The movement became global in 1993 when Clean Up Australia signed an agreement with the United Nations Environment Programme (UNEP) to manage and promote its programmes. The first Clean Up the World campaign took place in September 1993 and more than 30 million people in 80 countries participated in this community-based event. To date, some 40 million people from more than 120 countries in the world engage in cleaning up their streets, waters, parks and other areas (Clean Up Australia, website). In addition to organising national clean up days, Clean Up Australia under Ian Kiernan's skilful leadership is involved in a raft of projects and activities that centre on improving waste and resource management in Australia and abroad.

For his strong leadership and unwavering commitment to environmental causes, Ian Kiernan was named Australian of the Year in 1994, awarded the Order of Australia medal, and made an Officer of the Order of Australia in 1995. For his contribution to the environment internationally, he was made a United Nations Environment Programme Global 500 Laureate and was recipient of the prestigious United Nations Environment Programme Sasakawa Environment prize in 1998.

Some significant life forces for Ian Kiernan

Ian Kiernan was born in 1940 around the same time that his father went to war. During World War II, his father was a prisoner at Changi and endured the forced labour of making the infamous Burma Road. When he returned to Australia, his father was determined to get on with his life. Before the war he had studied at night school, learned a couple of languages and was stationed in London where he ran the buying office for GJ Coles. For Ian and his sister, this meant many years spent in boarding school. From the age of seven, Ian learned the valuable lesson of being able to get on with your mates and treasured the camaraderie that developed with a group of very good friends he continues to treasure.

After completing school, Ian worked for his father, who at this time owned an import/export business. As a 21-year-old, Ian toured the world but wasn't really happy in that line of work. The world of construction was more appealing to him. Ian left the family business and took a number of positions including a cadetship with a structural concrete and products company before he set up his own building business at the age of twenty-three, constructing factories and undertaking renovations. Starting small he then began buying property, including houses and a factory. Using his property management skills, he purchased old cottages in East Sydney, bringing them back to life and selling them for significant profits. At one time he had hundreds of terrace houses, not to mention four major blocks and a string of restaurants and personal assets including a house and boat. However, an increase in interest rates and problems with his business partner left him in a difficult financial situation. He responded by taking a year off, sailing to some of the most exotic islands in the world, much of the time spent solo. This episode in Ian's life, when he was experiencing a sense of incredible freedom, provided the impetus for him to compete in sailing competitions. Winning a single-handed trans-Tasman race gave him the spirit to confront the financial difficulties he had left behind. He reflects that, although it took twelve years, the business situation was settled and he was not made bankrupt. It was at this time, too, that Ian realised that there were more valuable things in life apart from money. One of these was, and continues to be, his love of the sea.

Two critical experiences have acted as catalysts for his crusade in environmental protection and preservation of oceans, both occurring during sailing competitions. The first of these was the influence of a fellow competitor who:

> encouraged us [the competitors from 11 nations in the world] … to hold our plastics on board to demonstrate to the 30,000 school kids that were studying the race … just how much plastic we might have thrown in the world's oceans and had not.

It is important to realise that at the time of the race, there were no international agreements about marine pollution or the dumping of plastics or other rubbish into the seas. Ian says this experience brought about a tremendous change in the way he viewed the oceans and challenged many ingrained practices he developed as a child that taught him it was perfectly natural and acceptable just to throw rubbish off the back of the boat.

A second and related experience was sailing through the Sargasso Sea, renowned for its golden seaweed, in the North Atlantic. As a child, Kiernan had read a fable about:

> an imaginary bird called the Halcyon bird [that] used to charm the sea to calm and come and land on the golden seaweed, lay its eggs and raise its fledglings.

Yet, the sight he witnessed was a stark and appalling contrast to this image.

> … huge clumps of golden seaweed, [scattered amongst it were items such as] a broken plastic bucket, a floating rubber thong … a plastic bag, a floating empty toothpaste tube, cigarette lighter.

> That [the witnessing of the marine pollution] was the trigger and I said, "Enough! When I get home I'm going to do something about Sydney harbour, my own backyard."

Ian's reaction of disgust propelled him to take action. Cleaning up Sydney harbour was his first project. Many others have followed.

Ian's vision

Ian Kiernan sees himself as

> an ordinary bloke who's made an environmental commitment to improve [his] environmental behaviour. (Kiernan in Top Achievers, n.d., p. 1).

Yet, Ian's achievements in the environmental field are significant in terms of their positive influence and impact. His germ of an idea has mobilised millions of people in more than 120 countries to be environmentally aware and pro-active.

Ian sees one of his qualities as having the ability to identify opportunities. As he says, "I've got a nose." This quality was evident in his early work as a property developer when he took a risk to redevelop terrace houses in suburbs around Sydney that were considered to be less than desirable at the time. Similarly, it was behind his highly successful idea for cleaning up and enlisting the moral and physical support of the general public. It was more successful than he imagined. He said that "nobody was more surprised than me to see the scale of that turnout on the first day".

He believes that the idea has been as successful because:

It's very wholesome, it's apolitical, it's not for profit and it's only got one agenda: that is to clean up and fix up ... It's not confrontational in a physical way. But at the same time, it is its own form of protest. Just by getting out there and cleaning up, people are protesting about the state of the environment in a positive proactive way. And it's owned by the people, we simply manage it for them. They own it. And we happened on a really good formula.

What Ian Kiernan has achieved so successfully in his campaign is to enlist many millions of people around the world to his vision, and to do this in tangible ways. People are engaged in very practical activities in cleaning up their environment. Yet, Clean Up is more than a one day a year event. It is an organisation that is involved in a variety of ongoing projects, some of which are small — a couple of thousand dollars in value — while others are up to $6 million dollars. Examples of such projects range from the clean up of rivers (such as Sydney Harbour, Derwent, Hawkesbury) to improving the waste management practices at Taronga Zoo.

Kiernan notes an important strategy of Clean Up is enlisting the interest and involvement of local communities to identify specific environmental and pollution problems. To give an example, he recalls that when the people of Wollongong and Port Kembla were concerned with the state of Lake Illawarra, a massive clean up event ensued. Among the rubbish emptied from this lake were 158 cars and 2 buses.

Another large-scale project in which Clean Up was involved was improving the waste management practices of Taronga Zoo. A lack of technology, an ageing infrastructure and poor work practices contributed to a situation where clean water was being used to hose out the animal cages. The moats and ponds where the animals swam and defecated were being emptied into Sydney Harbour. Talks with the management at the zoo and the local council were initiated and an agreement was struck that a better and more environmentally sound system was required. A chance meeting with a Danish company that had done work in the Soviet Union to treat the waterways that were affecting the fish and crayfish population proved successful because the company became a partner with Clean Up on this project. Clean Up raised over $2 million dollars to carry it out. Much of this was spent on infrastructure to develop a system of recycled water for the animals. Kiernan notes that he drove the project as though it were a construction project (which it was). Weekly meetings were held in the boardroom of the zoo and people present were given particular jobs to do. He described the outcome of the project as:

> we see the animals there in Taronga Zoo are swimming and drinking in a combination of their recycled effluent and recovered stormwater. And this is how you stop building another dam by more intelligent water management.

Ian Kiernan's vision for a better, cleaner environment, one that benefits not just one particular sector but many, has been translated into a range of highly successful, strategies across the last seventeen years. The Clean Up name and associated initiatives are widely known and respected, nationally and internationally. To achieve this, Ian has harnessed not only his only leadership capabilities, but those of others, drawing upon their resources to deliver his vision.

Ian's reflections on leadership

As Ian began to put his vision for the environment into practice by establishing Clean Up, he realised he needed to engage people from a broad cross-section of interests and expertise. Initially he sought help from influential friends and colleagues who had expertise in marketing and communications. He also consulted some prominent politicians to seek their endorsement of his ideas in principle. When the first politician approached did little to support his ideas, Ian did not give up, but simply sought the endorsement of another. Kiernan's motto is "I will not be beaten". A rejection from others makes him more determined and motivated to succeed. He explains that he thrives on the challenge. Looking back on his life, he sees a clear pattern taking on one challenge, and then another; each one becoming bigger and more complex.

Ian gives the impression that he is a servant leader. Not afraid to do the dirty work, he has attended over a hundred launches of Clean Up days in capital cities and regional towns throughout Australia. He meets and works with local people across many communities. Of these people, he says, "you give them a bit of a hand up [and] they paw the earth for you". He cites an example of a trip to Kimberley, Western Australia, where tourists behaving badly had contributed detrimentally to the natural environment. He said of that visit:

> I'm going to really lend them a hand. I've got to fly three-quarters of the way around Australia to do it, but I cannot not do it. And I guess that is leadership in itself.

Regarding his approach to leadership, Ian suggests in boating terms that:

> I think I lead from the front … I tend to put myself at the head of the column, but I think that probably comes from a practical background … you've got to be practical or else your boat sinks or you come last or both … A good boatman has a special standing there within the community because [others] know that he can or she can handle a boat in a difficult task of loading passengers or cargo or fishing or all the rest of it.

In Ian's view a leader is a person who has credibility in the eyes of their followers because he or she has the practical prowess, competence and reputation to do what needs to be done to achieve the goals and realise the vision.

The Board of Clean Up Australia has described Ian as *being* Clean Up Australia since he is its driving force. He is the pivotal figure who continues not only to set the vision, liaise with key players from governments of every persuasion both here and abroad, but also gets his hands dirty in the process. However, Ian suggests that his leadership strength, namely his personal drive and commitment, is also a weakness given potential threats to the long-term sustainability of the organisation if he continues to be seen as Mr Clean Up. Despite showing no signs of wishing to retire, Ian acknowledges that a succession strategy is a major challenge for the future, noting he needs to bring somebody in to work closely with him, learn the ropes and infiltrate the networks, so the legacy can be carried on.

An invaluable and unique leadership trait he brings to this organisation is a sophisticated ability to communicate his ideas to others, to engage them in the issue and to enlist their support whether it be in principle, in kind or via some other means. He also brings enthusiasm, a very infectious life-enhancing trait. At an Australia Day event Ian recalled a brief conversation he had with a former battalion command major who complimented him on winning Australian of the Year. The major said:

> … well, son, you are only showing me something that I've known for a long time and that is that if you have a good idea and you apply leadership you will find Australians will go anywhere, and do anything for you, that's what you've done.

Relationships with staff

While appearing to be Captain of the Clean Up Australia ship, Ian indicates that he is very much a team player who values the work and contribution of others. He uses terms such as mateship and peer respect to describe the relationships he has enjoyed with his staff in previous roles as well as in his current position as Chairperson of Clean Up Australia and Clean Up the World. He proudly refers to a strong, committed and enthusiastic team, comprising many young and talented graduates, all working towards the Clean Up vision.

Ian describes himself as an outgoing friendly sort of person. He values the people he works with and Clean Up is run as a team effort. He acknowledges that not all of the ideas for projects are his own, indicating he gets good ideas from forums, conferences, contacts and meeting "really smart people" who work for, and with, him. He sums up the positive working climate in his organisation by observing:

> We're doing all these ingenious inventive sort of things and having fun doing it ... we have a lot of humour ... I don't want to be a stony faced leader. I think I lead from the front, communicate well, but ... [I'm] ... a team player.

Since the inception of Clean Up Australia, Ian has developed many personal and powerful networks, consisting of not only treasured and influential friends, but also influential colleagues, many of whom are national and international political figures. It seems likely that without these significant partners and strong networks, Clean Up Australia and Clean Up the World may not have achieved to the extent they have. On the other hand, however, with such powerful allies, Clean Up is a powerful social and political player. In this regard, Ian notes that although the organisation does have power, they have to be careful how they use it and treat it with absolute respect. He recounts a story from a senior minister in the Federal Government who said:

> I have people coming into my office all the time with these grand plans and huge budgets. He [Kiernan] comes in and says, "Here's the plan, we're three-quarters of the way through it, I just need a bit more and can we do it?" I say "yes" and then it happens.

Learning

There is little doubt that much of Clean Up's success can be attributed to action learning principles, where people learn with, and from, each other. Under the driving vision of Ian Kiernan, engaging the right people at the right time in the various initiatives has been critical to the organisation's success. Along the way, Ian has drawn on his own earlier life's learnings, for example as a property developer, to facilitate and achieve positive environmental outcomes. He has also drawn on the knowledge and expertise of many others, many of whom have been attracted to the work and campaigns of Clean Up because of its national and international reputation.

Ongoing challenges

The environmental challenges facing the world today are enormous. Despite the work of people like Ian Kiernan and groups like Clean Up, these environmental challenges are unlikely to abate. Indeed, they seem to be growing in dimension and challenge as the world hurtles towards ever-greater consumerism and waste. Ian's view is that ignorance and greed are the two greatest contributors to environmental degradation. Yet his belief is that if we all rethink our behaviour and commit ourselves to improving the way we live in and respond to our environment, there is hope and a future. He remains optimistic and fiercely committed to the environmental cause despite being well aware of what would appear to be insurmountable global problems. He says:

> We [Clean up Australia] see it as our job to inspire communities — individuals, families, governments and businesses — to take responsibility and be actively involved in making their part of the world a cleaner and healthier place to live. (Kiernan in Clean Up Australia homepage, 2005, p. 1)

This ongoing and positive commitment to his environmental vision, despite the many challenges, remains the focus for Ian Kiernan's work.

Some important leadership learnings

→ Leaders must commit to a vision and be unrelenting in their drive to achieve this vision – they also may need to take a longer-term view to achieving their vision if ongoing challenges are evident (there is no "end" in some cases)

→ Leaders must engage and enlist others to achieving their vision – this may be required at multiple levels, from the general public, through to business and political sources

→ Leadership requires a vision, commitment, energy and passion

CHAPTER 10

Sarina Russo

Snapshot ...

→ Created the Office Business Academy in 1979 — this has evolved into one of Australia's largest, most successful and diverse training and employment entities (Sarina is Managing Director of Sarina Russo Job Access, Sarina Russo Schools | Australia, Russo Recruitment and James Cook University Brisbane — operated by Russo Higher Education)

→ Centenary Medal for service to education

→ Graduate of the Harvard Business School Owner/President Manager program

→ Co-author of *Meet me at the top*, a motivational book

Sarina is characterised by high energy, commitment and a drive to do better and be better in her business — she sets herself a vision and works tirelessly towards that vision.

Introductory profile

Sarina Russo established her business school, the Office Business Academy, in 1979, with only nine students. Today, after much hard work, her business employs approximately 700 staff with an annual turnover of $74 million (AUD). The Sarina Russo Group, of which she is Managing Director, now includes Sarina Russo Job Access, Sarina Russo Schools | Australia, Russo Recruitment, Russo Corporate Training, Sarina Investments and James Cook University Brisbane (operated by Russo Higher Education). Over 3000 students graduate annually from Sarina Russo Schools (Australia). Sarina Russo Job Access assists over 50,000 jobseekers each year into employment.

For her entrepreneurial achievements, Sarina has received accolades both in Australia and overseas. In 2003 she received the Centenary Medal for Distinguished Service to Education. In 2002 she was recognised as one of the world's forty leading women entrepreneurs. She has had a long association with the Harvard Business School where she is a member of the Women's Leadership Board of the John F. Kennedy School of Government. Sarina is a well-known public figure who has her own TV show, appears regularly on Australian radio and gives motivational lectures and seminars across the country. She is an expert business panellist on television, Channel Seven's "Dragon Den". Sarina is a member of a number of Boards and community groups, including Chairperson and Trustee of the Jupiter's Casino Community Benefit Fund (since 1995), member of the Queensland Premier's Business Advisory Board (since 2000) and member of the Council for Multicultural Australia Board (since 2005).

Some significant life forces for Sarina Russo

In Sarina's story, a range of life forces have played an important role in determining her character and leadership values and vision. A critical life force that has shaped her outlook and enabled her to become the successful business leader she is today comes from her Italian upbringing, particularly the influence of her father. Like so many migrants who settled in Australia post World War II, Sarina's parents saw this country as a land of opportunity that offered a bright and prosperous future for their children. Her father, a bridge worker and carpenter, instilled a strong work ethic in all of his children who were expected to devote weekends to the family businesses which included renting out apartments and working in the vineyard. As the youngest of the children and the one who stayed at home the longest, her father relied on Sarina to negotiate prices for the table grapes from the vineyard, deal with the produce market buyers and vendors and even see to evictions (Russo, 2002, p. 8). Sarina recalls that she was the only girl who attended All Hallows (a Catholic School for girls in Brisbane) who hated school holidays and hated weekends because she had to go to the farm and work. Yet, there were some valuable lessons Sarina gleaned from working with her father.

> He gave me my valuable strengths — the capacity to endure
> hard work and confidence in myself ... [he] had equipped me
> to face any challenge with optimism and commitment. He
> also taught me the value of saving and the basic business skills
> which have got me where I am today. (Russo, 2002, p. 115)

While she paid great tribute to the influence of her father and to a loving family background, she also referred to "feelings of being enslaved by ... family duties" (p. 9) which included handing over half of her wage to her parents and working all of her spare time in the family businesses. The desire to remain single and lead an independent life was also at odds with her family's beliefs about a woman's rightful place in the world. These formative experiences made her determined to break away from her family's restrictive cultural mores and seek a life of personal and financial independence; a life less ordinary. She ran away at the age of twenty-six to find her own destiny.

Sarina says she suffered many setbacks when trying to establish herself — particularly people telling here she couldn't do certain things. However, she was determined and lived out, and still lives out, her motto, "It can be done".

Sarina's vision

There is little doubt that Sarina is a leader who embodies vision, passion, incredible conviction and commitment. She speaks of the importance of having a vision and working hard with, and through, others to see that vision move from being a shared vision to a set of tangible outcomes. Her motto drives her to achieve. Her decision to establish a commercial training college with no prior experience of establishing or operating one, little formal education, little capital and considerable opposition from family and friends did not deter her (Russo, 2002). In some respects, Sarina's decision to pursue such a business venue was a swim against the tide, where she avoided the negative reactions of her critics as well as some of her friends. Sarina could well be describing herself when she said:

> ... a leader is an individual who is going somewhere, heading to,
> or pointing to, new horizons. Leaders have visionary qualities that
> draw others along with them toward a declared destination or
> goal. They may lead from in front – or, as shepherds, they may
> guide from behind. (Russo, 2002, p. 127)

Sarina states that her ultimate vision when she started a business was to keep growing it as well as herself, by constant learning and challenging herself to do more (Russo, 2002). Some twenty-five years ago she certainly did not foresee herself as Managing Director of the multi-million dollar group of companies she heads up now. In large part, Sarina's success seems to be due to her long-term vision and commitment to see the businesses succeed. Interestingly, she says that:

> It is still important to set a long-term strategy but because so much change is happening [in the world] it is now equally important to strategise on a weekly, monthly and yearly basis. (Russo, 2002, p. 182)

Responding to current events is critical in her business, such as the challenges thrown up some years ago by the SARS threat. For example, the education market's vulnerability to wider global forces was evident in 2003 when Sarina decided to refuse Chinese education tours to Australia because of the risk of the spread of SARS. This decision cost the business one million dollars in revenue. While this could be construed as a setback, Sarina was not fazed. As she said, the volatile overseas market would drive her company more strongly into the domestic market. For every crisis, Sarina is able to see an opportunity.

Two of her characteristics are a strong self-belief and the confidence to proceed in the face of adversity. Not long after she established her commercial college, she fought hard with the relevant authorities to get the courses accredited. It took many appointments and much persuasive talking with the officers in charge before the courses were recognised (Russo, 2002). It took months of negotiations. In the third year of operation the building in which the Office was located caught fire. This setback meant that Sarina had to find new premises (Russo, 2002, pp. 41–42). After the fire, Sarina said:

> I was devastated but I rose above the challenges because I wanted it [the business] so badly and I wanted to continue on leading and doing what I really was passionately excited about.

Sarina moved to a more prestigious location and ten years later, purchased her first building. Even buying a building became a challenge as few real estate agents in Brisbane were willing to take her seriously. Sarina claims the reason for their reluctance was due to her being a woman (Russo, 2002). Back in the early 1990s in Australia, it was atypical for a woman to demonstrate entrepreneurial activity on such a large scale. Sarina believes that, in many ways, her drive for financial independence has made her a pioneer for other women. As she says:

> [for] ... women today their biggest motivation is financial independence. Women today have got more drive in starting their own businesses because they ... want ... financial independence. They want this freedom, they want these choices ... So today it's not just getting married and getting the house, they can buy their own house.

Thinking about what drives her towards achieving her vision, Sarina feels that she will never lose the passion for what she does:

> ... because your goals get bigger and so your commitment is just as strong ... So my passion is not going to die.

Sarina's reflections on leadership

> Leadership is definitely not something that you're born with. I think leadership is something that you acquire ... we can all become leaders and it depends on how your environment allows you to do it.

Sarina believes that leaders are products of their environment, shaped by it and shapers of it. For her, the strong work ethic she inherited from her father and her desire for financial independence pushed her in a particular direction. Being unable to hold down several secretarial positions, because she "wanted to run the show", coupled with her great desire for financial and personal independence, fuelled her determination to become self-employed. From very humble beginnings her training business expanded and with each passing year she had more opportunities to embrace new challenges and diversify aspects of it. For example, in 1998 she extended the activities of the business by taking on the challenge of operating Job Network which provides job matching, assistance for long-term unemployed and job search training activities. Her institute of training and job network agency continue to meet a growing need in the marketplace and economy.

The specific environmental context in which Sarina chose to immerse herself is significant and reveals something of her interests and priorities. Her first-hand experiences of being unemployed, a short yet successful stint at teaching typewriting at a commercial college, and a strong desire to be in a position where she could have more autonomy and choice over her life were key drivers in the establishment of a business providing training and employment for job seekers. Given her experiences, the focus of a business in the field of training for job seekers was not unexpected.

> I know what it was like when I didn't have a job, when I didn't have an education ... And I feel that I had to go through the tough times in my twenties to be able to empathise with people.

The Office, as it was called in the early days, provided an important space for Sarina to develop not only a successful training and recruitment business, but also a suite of leadership and management skills that would hold her in good stead as she continued to expand the business and take on more challenges. She admits quite openly that she developed the skills of leadership through experience (Russo, 2002).

> Leadership is all about creating certainty when really you are feeling internally uncertain. Leadership is about feeling certain when your environment is uncertain, leadership is about leading with certainty though you're doubting your decision.

Sarina indicates that an important role for leaders is to provide a climate of certainty and security within their organisations. While the rest of the world is characterised by chaos and change, the organisation needs to be a safe and certain haven. According to Sarina, when leaders themselves exude confidence and demonstrate a strong degree of self-control, then they are setting a climate of certainty (Russo, 2002).

She sees leadership as something embedded deeply, organisationally and interwoven with the people of the organisation. However, Sarina recognises that being a leader can sometimes be very lonely, even though there are some wonderful rewards. Because of her prominent role in her organisations, and the high expectations she sets for herself and her colleagues, she sees it as her:

> responsibility ... [to] ... stay sharp and alert and no one ever sees me unenthusiastic or demotivated ... So if I'm exhausted, I'll take time out and then people will always see me refreshed. They will never see me in a demotivated state.

Relationships with staff

Sarina points out that she works as a member of a team, relying heavily on others, particularly her managers, to help her do the job:

as a leader ... I have to listen to (name) because (name) is more hands on to what's happening.

An important lesson she learned at the Harvard Business School was that staff are your drive, your energy, your most valuable asset. You have to know how to choose them well, how to switch them on and keep them switched on (Russo, 2002). Motivating and empowering staff to achieve their personal best is a key role Sarina sees for leadership (Russo, 2002). Not only does she reward good performance with bonus payments, but she also acknowledges high performing staff at meetings and in a myriad of other ways.

Critical to her leadership is surrounding herself with excellent staff who can complement her strengths.

I find people who can fill my weaknesses and then we've got a great team ... Team is very, very important ... I work with a great team of people and I rely on them to drive certain parts of the business. But ultimately I realise that it's my responsibility.

Although Sarina proclaims that the team is key, it is evident that her leadership style is one where she remains closely connected to all facets of the business. Her stamp is indelibly marked on her organisation's activities.

Sarina speaks of the importance of having staff who share her work ethic and values (Russo, 2002) and staff who fit in to the organisation's vision and mission. She says that with her management and financial people, she "speak [s] ...[her] truth to them and they speak theirs to ... [her]" (Russo, 2002, p. 133). Yet for staff who are under-performing or do not fit in Sarina refers to the need for decisive action:

... you have to do something about it. Not just for the sake of your business but for the sake of the people in the organisation who may suffer through your inaction. (Russo, 2002, p. 130)

Sarina sets very high expectations for staff, particularly her managers. She expects her managers to show commitment "... not just of 99 per cent, not 100 percent, but 110 per cent" (Russo, 2002, p. 156). To help them carry out their work, she provides specialist one-on-one coaching. For these staff, she plays a key role in coaching them in the ways of entrepreneurship and invests heavily in their education. In regard to entrepreneurship, Sarina states that she encourages them to buy property, teaches them how to apply for and manage loans and introduces them to her bankers. The overall aim is to help them achieve their financial dreams and become more financially secure. For these staff also, she subsidises further study at James Cook University Brisbane or sends them to the Harvard Business School or other Schools in the United States. She tries to encourage her senior staff to study or do whatever has helped her. In the same way, she expects her senior staff to energise their people through their passion and commitment (Russo, 2002). Over the years, Sarina has turned to her management team not only for their perspectives on how to improve the business, but also to challenge her thinking about particular practices (Russo, 2002).

An important professional relationship Sarina values highly is the longstanding business association she has had with her brother-in-law, a lawyer. Since the early days of starting the business, he has been a key figure who has acted as a confidant, mentor, coach and ally:

> I could never have got where I have without his presence in the business and the wisdom, advice and guidance he has imparted ... [he] has been a pillar of strength and a mentor to me. (Russo, 2002, p. vi)

Learning

Sarina refers to the importance of engaging in formal learning activities to help her become a more credible and knowledgeable leader. This is despite the significant learnings she has gained as part of her life experiences and the need to learn as she went along, especially in the early years of the growth of her businesses.

> ... I realised that I needed to educate myself because I was struggling in learning to become a manager and a businessperson because ... I didn't necessarily have the skills as a leader ... as my business grew and grew and grew I then decided ... that I had to educate myself.

She is a great advocate of lifelong learning and education. She notes that she has never stopped learning or reading books. Failing junior English once and senior English twice (as a mature student) did not quash her enthusiasm or desire to continue to learn as much as she could about operating an effective business. She recognised early in the life of her business that she did not have the requisite leadership and financial skills so she sought them elsewhere. For the past ten years she has participated in courses provided by the Harvard Business School and completed Harvard's Owner/President Management course. Aside from formal university study, Sarina has improved her knowledge by attending motivational seminars and engaging in reading (in particular, biographies of famous leaders).

Ongoing challenges

Sarina's strong sense of commitment to what she does, and her drive to seek new challenges do not seem to have waned, despite her being in business for over twenty-six years. She says that leadership is a 24-hour a day job and she is:

> more passionate today than I was yesterday, last week, last month, last year, because I've got more to lose. I'm very driven … now to maintain the dynamics of this company. That's my driving force.

She sees her drive for expanding her property portfolio as a means to give her company leverage against her business should some part of it fail.

In reflecting on those she admires as leaders and those she uses to illustrate points she makes, it is clear that her benchmarks for, and models of, success are people who have achieved most highly in world business and political sectors. In looking to these people, and setting her own challenges, she is confident of success because "it can be done".

Some important leadership learnings

→ Leaders must be vision-driven, working with high energy, passion and commitment towards that vision

→ Leadership is about not accepting challenges and barriers to achieving the vision, but findings solutions to achieving the desired outcomes

→ Building quality teams — where team members are committed to the vision and where they complement each other's skills — is critical

→ Learning is a lifelong journey, addressed through formal as well as informal ways

---

CHAPTER 11

Maggi Sietsma

Snapshot ...

→ Founder/artistic director of Expressions Dance Company, Brisbane

→ Previously with Australian Ballet, London Festival Ballet and Theatre du Chêne Noir (France)

→ Expressions won the Sidney Myer Arts Award, 1997

→ Developed the first Bachelor of Arts (Dance) course in Queensland

→ Order of Australia, 2002

→ Churchill Fellowship winner, 2003

Maggi is characterised by passion, commitment and energy toward achieving her vision of innovative dance. Her creativity, drive and strong sense of self-belief have transformed much conventional thinking about contemporary dance.

Introductory profile

As a child, a life-changing event for Maggi Sietsma was seeing Dame Margot Fonteyn dance. The experience ignited a lifetime interest and passion for this art form. Unlike many little girls who just dream of becoming prima ballerinas, Maggi achieved her dream. Due to her extraordinary talent, she performed on stage not only with Margot Fonteyn, but also other greats such as Rudolf Nureyev and Sir Robert Helpmann. As a 16-year old she was granted a scholarship to study with any dance school in the world. She was one of only three graduates of the Australian Ballet who received an offer to join the company, and she achieved her ambition of becoming a soloist. She was soloist with two prestigious ballet companies: the London Festival Ballet and the Avignon Opera Ballet. Because of her ability and classical training, she was the first Westerner to be offered a scholarship to study Indonesian Classical Dance at the Kraton (Palace) in Jogjakarta. Yet it was at the pinnacle of her career that she decided to take a different direction in dance. Her foray into the field of contemporary dance saw her work for an avant-garde French theatrical company and not long after, she and a group of like-minded artists created their own music and dance multi-media ensemble, Muance, which toured major cities in Europe (Expressions Dance Company, n.d.). In Muance, she played a major directorial role not only as choreographer but also as manager.

In the early 1980s Maggi, her partner and small child returned to Australia. With her European experience, she was inundated with offers of work. She decided to take the position as resident choreographer with an amateur (or pro-am) ballet company in North Queensland. During her one-year stay, she prepared the groundwork for the company's transition to professional status. Today, this company is the well-known group, Dance North. Following this experience, Maggi and her family moved to Brisbane which has been her base ever since. She taught modern dance at Brisbane College of Advanced Education (now the Queensland University of Technology) and some years later established the professional contemporary dance company, Expressions Dance Company. As artistic director of Expressions, Maggi Sietsma has received many accolades both nationally and internationally for her choreographic work. Prominent among these is the Sidney Myer Performing Arts Award. In 2002, Maggi was appointed a member of the Order of Australia for services to dance and dance education. She is currently Dean of Dance at the Hong Kong Academy of Performing Arts (Expressions Dance Company, n.d.). In 2006 she was included as one of the Advance 100 Global Australians (for the Arts) by *The Australian* newspaper.

Since its inception in the mid 1980s, Expressions has grown from being a germ of an idea to a company with a million dollar budget. Its company of performers have received standing ovations in countries from New York to Beijing and today the company continues to perform original works all over the world. Expressions is renowned for creating works that push the boundaries between dance and theatre, where both speech and visual media can be found. It has a well-earned reputation for its energy, risk-taking and originality.

Some significant life forces for Maggi Sietsma

A significant life force in Maggi's life was her first teacher, her mother, who grew up in Indonesia. Her mother spent four years of her life from the age of sixteen to twenty in a prison camp during World War II.

After the war, she married and then lived with her family in Singapore and Malaysia for just over a decade. At the age of forty, Maggi's mother realised she wanted to be more than a homemaker, so she completed her HSC and then attended university. She graduated as a psychologist and worked for many years in the Education Department where she was involved in the diagnostic assessment of children. Maggi admires her mother's courage and determination to break away from her socially conventional role of housewife to become qualified and take up a new and satisfying career. Given that she had received little formal education as a young person, and that a portion of her life was interrupted by the horrors of war, Maggi acknowledges that her mother showed incredible resilience and was a great inspiration to her.

In addition to being a strong role model, Maggi's mother was also critical in immersing Maggi into the world of dance and movement. During her time in Singapore, Maggi says her mother was:

> always terribly interested in directing — she was a swimming teacher ... and I grew up with my mother creating water ballets and putting on concerts and performances for the swimming club.

Her mother helped her to see that:

> ... anyone could ... [put on shows] ... and I never assumed that I would not do it myself ... My mother always instilled ... in me [that] you can do whatever you want.

It is a strong sense of belief in herself and her abilities, coupled with the notion that people can change the course of their own lives, that govern her life and work as a dancer and as a creative leader of dance.

Another critical life force for Maggi was during 1972 when, working as a classical dancer, she attended a performance by the Nederlands Dans Theater. This contemporary group "blew [her] ... socks off" because of its energy, vibrancy and innovation in dance. It was a stark contrast to the conventional world of classical dance that she knew and inhabited. An offer for her to work with the company saw Maggi leave the Australian Ballet Company and head overseas. In the end she did not dance with the Dutch company, but joined the

London Festival Ballet. While she was appointed soloist with the company — one of her lifetime ambitions — she felt emotionally torn as the contemporary dance world was also beckoning. The experience of being a dancer with a theatre company in France, as well as choreographing works for a company which she helped to establish, provided further opportunities for her to enmesh herself in the world of contemporary dance where she felt most at home.

Maggi's vision

As a child, Maggi passionately wanted to be a dancer, predicting she would achieve her life goal by 1972. Her prediction came true and in 1972 she was employed as a dancer with the Australian Ballet Company. Yet as the years passed and even after achieving the accolade of promotion to soloist in two overseas companies, not an easy feat in such an elitist and competitive world, she came to question her original vision and what she wanted most in her life.

> I actually got very disillusioned with ballet companies, the hierarchical structure really didn't suit my personality. I … found that I was being treated like a child and [I] didn't respect that sort of approach.

Her love of dancing never left her but she was inspired to seek different styles and techniques of creative movement and dance including Balinese dancing, Tai Chi, and contemporary dance. She explains that as the only dancer in the Theatre Du Chêne Noir, she had to redefine what her dance was because she was suddenly all alone. No one was directing her. She comments that the company worked so well because it was based on collaboration and mutual respect amongst the artists (the musicians, actors and dancer). It was a contrast to the hierarchical structures characteristic of classical ballet companies.

That Maggi went on to establish her own dance company in Queensland, Australia, was not surprising, given her previous dancing and choreography experience and the success of her French-based dance and music company, Muance. Establishing her company was not without its challenges, as many people, including government officials, endeavoured to dissuade her since there were already two such companies there. Not a person to back away from her ideas and vision, she persisted and Expressions Dance Company was born. The main reason Maggi set up a company in Queensland was due to need. While teaching dance at Brisbane College of Advanced Education in the early

1980s, Maggi became concerned that there were very few, if any, employment opportunities for graduates in modern dance. It was this thought that propelled her to establish a company that would employ some of the graduates.

For the first three years of the company's life, Maggi continued to work full-time as a lecturer in dance at BCAE and devoted most nights and all weekend to getting shows and projects together. The schedule was quite gruelling. She remembers that she didn't take a wage from Expressions for the first three years and when she did receive a salary, it was 60 per cent below what she had earned as a tertiary teacher. Unlike a lot of other small companies that are based on profit share, Maggi was determined to see the company become professional and offer its dancers a salary and decent work conditions. So committed was Maggi to see the company succeed, that she and her partner:

> mortaged [their] house for the first season of Expressions ... gave up everything to work in Expressions and gladly ... because that's where my heart was, still in the profession.

Maggi promotes dance through a range of educational programs and forums throughout Queensland and overseas. She recalls, along with other like-minded colleagues, battling hard to ensure that dance became a curriculum area for high school students. Expressions is also pro-active in the education field through master classes, offered both in Australia and overseas. Every time Expressions tours, it provides master classes and choreographic workshops. Maggi stresses that she has been very pro-active in order to develop dance literacy in the country, and that has to start with education.

Maggi's reflection on leadership

As a child and teenager Maggi found herself in positions where she was out in front, setting examples for her peers, and teaching, guiding and directing them. In school, she was a class captain, inspiring and leading her fellow students. She also shone outside the classroom, on the sports field and in the school concert hall. Maggi was a gifted sportsperson, excelling in all sports. She represented her high school in many competitive activities and was responsible for choreographing school musicals, no doubt influenced by her mother's early involvement in choreography and creative movement.

Dance provided an outlet where she could continue to exercise her leadership abilities.

> When I was 14, I ran my own dance studio, and had 200 students and put them through the Royal Academy of Dance examinations. I inherited that studio from my original ballet teacher … I would put on the annual concerts and do all the work required to achieve that. My mother helped out taking all the fees … I had three staff members. I had two assistants and a pianist …

At this time, Maggi was engaged in intense training for advanced dance examinations herself in addition to doing her school work and participating actively in school sporting and cultural events. She coped successfully with this huge workload, achieving 100 per cent success rates for her students and achieving outstanding grades for her own performance. Here, she demonstrated a capacity to not only develop her own capabilities, but also to support and facilitate the development of those in others. She is a tenacious person and believes strongly that people can change the course of their lives.

There were a number of times in Maggi's life when she abandoned performing in order to pursue other activities. After she left the Festival Ballet in London, Maggi returned to Australia where she taught Tai Chi at the Gita School of Yoga in Melbourne. At this time, she stumbled into a Handicraft of Asia shop one day, secured a part-time job and within three weeks became the manager. Some years later, a move to Brisbane saw Maggi take up a full-time job in the tertiary sector where she was employed to teach dance. In all of these situations, Maggi was not fazed by the new challenges; on the contrary they allowed her to broaden her experience and to exercise her leadership skills and abilities in a variety of contexts.

As a director, Maggi sees herself essentially as a decision maker; decisions which require problem-solving skills. She gives the example of an idea she had for the production of her work, *Flight*, that involved the creative use of a balloon. She spoke to her production manager who said that the idea was impossible in practice. That weekend Maggi purchased some balloons and found a way to make the idea work. She says of herself, "I just don't take no for an answer unless people can really prove it to me … I guess that's part of my nature." Another time she organised a "walkout" for the dancers at the London Festival Ballet. She was the ring leader who instigated the action in protest against the way she and the other dancers had been treated.

On reflecting on leadership outside the world of dance, Maggi admires people "who have real strength of purpose ... and a real drive and determination to achieve their goals".

Relationships with staff

In talking about the process of creating and choreographing a work, Maggi notes that while:

> it's a collaborative thing ... there has to be one vision ultimately and I think ... one of my skills is the fact that I can get together a whole group of people and give them enough confidence, trust, and responsibility to contribute to the work, to my vision. But ultimately, it is my vision that they get behind.

She recalls an example of a collaborative venture that saw Expressions and the City Contemporary Dance Company from Hong Kong perform a new programme. She comments that the task of trying to draw all of the dancers and ideas together and to manage all those egos and keep them all happy was very challenging indeed, but not impossible; it is a role that is central to her work as artistic director. Part of this work is motivating and exciting the dancers by taking them along the journey of creating art.

Maggi believes she has very good and long-lasting relationships with staff, from the technical team through to the dancers, as well as other artists with whom she collaborates. Since the early days of Expressions, Maggi has worked with many dancers, some of whom have stayed with her anywhere between four and nine years. During this time, only four people have left the company under a cloud. When she can, she tries to advise and support dancers who previously worked for her by helping them move in other directions and explore other fields of endeavour. She gave the example of a dancer who had been with her for nine years who wanted to transition from being a performer but was scared to find himself unemployed with a family to feed. At this time, Maggi had been offered a position in a dance course in Singapore. As she did not want the position she recommended that her protégé be given it. The outcome was very positive and he took the job gladly. In part, this illustrates much of what is central to Maggi's work; that is, the loyal and trusting relationships she forges and develops with her dancers.

She attributes her easygoing style and sense of humour to her success in being able to work with many different personalities. Of the dancers, she says they

> feel quite comfortable working with me, they trust me ... they know where the boundaries are ... We can have a

> laugh and have fun but when we get down to work we get
> *down to work* [our emphasis] … but ultimately, I have to
> take the responsibility.

Another element central to the effective functioning of working with
the dancers is the need for enjoyment. Maggi believes that without
enjoyment, there is little purpose in dance. It would seem that most
dancers and other non-commercial artists engage in their art for the
sheer love of it since, as Maggi pointed out, they get so poorly paid.

Maggi's creative work sees her collaborating with other artists such
as actors, directors and musicians. Another important collaborative
relationship is with her partner, Abel Valls, who contributes both to the
managerial and creative side of Expressions (Clarke, 2005). Maggi
suggests that she could not have achieved her vision to set up a professional contemporary dance company without his strong support,
creative artistry, and steadying influence.

Learning

Maggi is a firm believer in the power and value of education. In
addition to completing a Master of Arts in dance in the mid 1990s, an
important source of her learning has been several intercultural
exchanges to countries including China, India, Papua New Guinea,
Mexico, and the United States. During these times she has taught
dance, developed dance curriculum materials and choreographed works
for overseas companies. An exciting opportunity was her stay at the
Beijing Academy where she taught for six weeks and helped the staff
develop a contemporary dance curriculum.

> I love intercultural exchange because I think it's only at the
> human level that we can really grow and develop, and it is by
> learning from those other cultures that we can develop some
> real harmony in this very difficult world.

Maggi conveys that, for her, working with others in achieving her goals is
both an artistic journey as well as a learning one. She also admits: "I
think honestly, I'm really fascinated and interested in people."

Ongoing challenges

An ongoing challenge that Expressions and other similar smaller
performing arts organisations continue to face is a lack of sufficient
funding and recognition of the work they do by government and other
bodies. This situation causes Maggi much frustration.

> ... it's fatiguing running a company the way I have to on a shoestring ... I'm really bored I have to say, with writing submissions for increased funding and having to continually justify why the company deserves to exist.

On occasions, financial issues have been such that Maggi has had to reduce the number of dancers employed. One of the hardest things she has had to endure is asking staff to leave because of budget constraints. Another source of frustration, and an ongoing challenge, is the mismatch between the number of dance graduates in Australia and the number of available jobs for dancers. She explains that universities continue to graduate dancers who are unlikely to get work here. This challenge is connected with the lack of long-term future development in the arts in Australia. She adds:

> There are probably, in any one year, in the non-commercial dance scene, not more than 5 jobs going in the country. It's shocking ... It's horrible.

Despite this, Expressions has over the years, been a major employer of student graduates. Ideally, she said she would like to see dance graduates become high school teachers. She believes in this way, they would get employment and "teach people to appreciate the art form so that we can continue to develop audiences".

There is a strong sense that Maggi Sietsma still has much to achieve in the world of dance. As she says:

> In terms of my own creativity ... I do believe that I've still got my best years to come really ... [and in the longer term] I'd like to see the company continue to grow when I leave.

Some important leadership learnings

→ Leaders need to be driven by a passionate and unerring commitment to a vision, accepting there may be many barriers and challenges in achieving that vision

→ Learning is a lifelong journey, drawing on the opportunities — successful and otherwise, expected and different — that people experience

→ Leadership draws on creativity, risk taking and a capacity to lead and develop others in collaborative ventures

CHAPTER 12

Some important
leadership learnings

Our ten stories provide unique and powerful insights into how some outstanding Australians think about, and practise, leadership. What we would like to stress is how different our leaders are — in background, life experiences as well as in their fields of endeavour. However, as we prepared the draft chapters for this book, we came to feel that our remarkable subjects were writing a textbook on leadership as their stories provided real-life illustrations of leadership in action.

We have endeavoured to capture some of the key leadership insights and practices of our leaders via a summary table provided at the end of each chapter (i.e. *Some important leadership learnings*). We now offer a further brief analysis of these leadership learnings by utilising the lens provided by Kouzes and Posner's *Leadership Challenge* framework as outlined in Chapter 1. The discussion here draws together and highlights some of the theoretical underpinnings of our leaders' stories, framed around Kouzes and Posner's five leadership practices.

In Chapter 1 we noted that the first of these practices, *modelling the way*, related to leaders drawing on and practising their own values, beliefs and principles. Leaders set examples by aligning these values and their actions.

It was evident that each of the ten leaders modelled the way, whether it was through words or actions. Each of them was very clear about what they stood for, what they expected of themselves and what they expected of others. Despite the fact that Michael Kirby took a highly critical view of leadership (particularly in the political domain), there was no doubt that from the broader leadership views he expressed and from the examples drawn from his own practices, he was deeply committed to social justice and humanitarian principles. He was not alone here as other leaders, for example, Tim Costello, Jim Soorley and Linda Burney, articulated similar values and beliefs. Jim Soorley put it bluntly, arguing that leaders must believe in something and combine this with a commitment to work hard with understanding and compassion.

All of the ten leaders demonstrated considerable modesty in their conversations with us, given their prominence, exceptional achievements and Australia-wide distinction. Despite this, it was evident that they were certainly *modelling the way*, whether it was for those with whom they worked closely, or others less directly associated with their work. They each demonstrated levels of excellence in their endeavours, providing clear and unambiguous *models* of their values, beliefs and visions.

This notion of vision leads on to the next leadership practice, *inspiring a shared vision*. For some of the ten leaders, this was possibly the most significant of all the five practices, where they were strongly and overtly committed to a vision, pursuing it with belief and considerable enthusiasm. This was coupled with an awareness that they needed to enlist others to be effective. For Sarina Russo this was paramount. She argued that leaders must be vision-driven and committed to it by way of high energy and passion. These notions were echoed by Maggi Sietsma who looked to unerring commitment as a key driver for leaders. Jim Soorley and Ian Kiernan also recognised the importance of leaders engaging others if they want to achieve their desired outcomes. Fiona Wood and Christine Nixon reiterated these notions, seeing leadership (and teamwork) as driven by passion and commitment to strive for excellence, and in Fiona Wood's case, to answer the difficult questions in the field of medical research. Michael Kirby raised some cautions regarding the need to learn from the lessons of history — leaders may have a vision but they can choose to act for evil as well as for good.

The search for answers to difficult questions leads seamlessly to the next leadership practice, *challenge the process,* where leaders seek innovative ways to change and improve, by taking risks and learning from mistakes. Peter Doherty likened this practice to a journey of discovery. Christine Nixon created new paths for women leaders in an organisation dominated by a strong male culture. Maggi Sietsma's ideas highlighted that one of the realities of leadership in action was accepting there might be barriers and challenges and that leadership draws on creativity and risk taking. Indeed, many of the leaders spoke of leadership as a learning journey. Sarina Russo argued that leadership was not about accepting challenges and barriers to achieving the vision, but ought to focus on finding solutions to these to achieve one's goals. Ian Kiernan suggested that we might need to take a longer-term view to achieving our vision, if ongoing challenges are evident. His leadership story continues to be filled with challenges and obstacles. Linda Burney reminded us that in the quest for achieving one's vision, there might be a personal cost, and her story provided a sobering reality check for this leadership practice.

Linda Burney also argued that leadership was not a sole activity. It draws on, and develops from, others. This is the fourth leadership practice, *enabling others to act.* Here, leaders need to understand that achieving one's vision is a team effort. Such teams are built on collaboration, trust and strong relationships. In this regard, Jim Soorley argued that leaders need to draw on the skills, knowledge and capabilities of others to build a quality team. Ego should have no place and the best and brightest talents must be included as leadership team members. Fiona Wood echoed these sentiments, seeing leadership as a team-based approach. Peter Doherty similarly believed that genuine collegiality and respect for all team members was critical in achieving outcomes. Sarina Russo saw the value in building quality teams, where team members were committed to the vision and where they complemented each others' skills; a notion similar to that of Jim Soorley. Finally, and emphasising the significance of empowering others and fostering collaboration and teamwork, Ian Kiernan argued that enlisting others may be required at multiple levels to achieve the vision.

The fifth leadership practice, *encouraging the heart,* requires that leaders recognise the achievements and contributions of others — people are valued and successes are celebrated. Of all the five leadership practices, this one was less evident, at least in an overt sense, among the ten leaders. However, it is embedded more broadly in the focuses the leaders identified as critical underpinnings of successful leadership — people and relationships. Perhaps this reflects the focus of our questioning during the interviews. Perhaps it reflects a cultural matter, whereby success is often tempered by modesty and humbleness.

Kouzes and Posner's five leadership practices provided a useful way to draw together many of the key themes to emerge from this journey of discovery based on the lives and leadership stories of ten distinguished Australians. However, as well as these five practices, there are other matters that all leaders (and aspiring leaders) may need to consider as they reflect on their own leadership.

The first of these concerns *learning* — that is, that leaders need to see themselves as learners. Maggi Sietsma and Tim Costello see this in terms of developing as a leader from critical life forces, experiences and opportunities taken. Peter Doherty and Fiona Wood both refer to learning as a journey of enquiry and discovery, driven by research. Other leaders such as Sarina Russo and Christine Nixon refer to the value of formal learning that enhanced their learning about leadership. For Christine Nixon, a key aspect of her learning was undertaking formal study in another country such that she was able to later draw into her work ideas from other fields. The second relates to working towards a *vision that is concerned with creating a better future*. This more holistic purpose of leadership is made by Tim Costello and echoed by Linda Burney; both of whom point out that leadership is a moral process. Ian Kiernan suggests there is no end to leadership if the challenges are ongoing. The third refers to leaders *accepting responsibility*. Both Michael Kirby and Peter Doherty argue this point, urging that leaders must accept responsibility and accountability — and must know when to go. Indeed, Peter Doherty argues that some leaders may need to be pushed, if they do not see it is time for them to go. The fourth relates to the very powerful *social justice principles* driving some of the leaders. In part this may reflect the individuals we studied. It may also reflect the particular fields of endeavour from which the leaders come. Notwithstanding this, for Linda Burney, Jim Soorley, Tim Costello and Michael Kirby, such orientations to leadership are paramount. They argue for leaders to show empathy and to commit to social justice, equity and human rights. For Linda Burney, leadership is also embedded in notions of humbleness, respect, loyalty and decency.

In consideration of the ideas highlighted above, there are a number of overall messages and learnings to take from the leadership stories of our ten remarkable Australians.

- Leadership is not a concept to be considered simplistically nor in isolation — it is not to be defined by a formula nor can we propose a recipe for its development. Leadership takes many forms, is understood in different ways and enacted in different contexts. Despite this, there are a number of commonalities that can be brought to our understandings.

- How leaders talk about leadership, how they understand its nuances and its practice is deeply embedded in their own life forces and experiences, their personal values, beliefs and driving principles and the fields of endeavour in which they work.

- Leadership must be about something! It must be vision-driven, it must enliven commitment and passion not only within the leader, but also among those with whom the leader works. We need to be reminded that leadership can have both good intentions and otherwise — we need to be aware of the leadership lessons of history.

- Leadership is an ongoing journey. It is not easy, being constantly confronted by challenges and barriers. Risk taking and creativity are often required to achieve the vision. Commitment and conviction are mandatory.

- Leadership is not a singular activity — leading with and through others is not rhetoric, but reality.

- Leaders need to be accountable, while at the same time demonstrating understanding and compassion in the drive to do better tomorrow than today.

This journey into leadership has been a fascinating and enriching one for us as researchers and writers. Listening to each Australian story has provided us with a valuable opportunity to rethink our personal and academic views about leadership. The stories have enhanced and enlightened our understanding and left us humbled by the depth of commitment and drive our ten leaders displayed. There is little doubt that they are ten outstanding Australians. Our final reflection is what might we have learned had we included leaders from different fields such as a sporting leader, a voluntary community leader, a youth leader? Perhaps these are questions for another leadership book.

References

Chapter 1

Bass, B. M. (1981). *Stogdill's handbook on leadership.* New York: Free Press.

Bass, B. M. (1985). *Leadership and performance beyond expectations.* New York: Free Press.

Bernard, L. L. (1926). *An introduction to social psychology.* New York: Holt.

Blount, F., & Joss, B. (with D. Mair). (1999). *Managing in Australia.* Sydney, Australia: Lansdowne.

Burns, J. M. (1978). *Leadership.* New York: Harper & Row.

Fiedler, F. E. (1967). *A theory of leadership effectiveness.* New York: McGraw-Hill.

Drath, W. H., & Palus, C. J. (1994). *Making common sense: Leadership as meaning-making in a community of practice.* Greensboro, NC: Center for Creative Leadership.

Dubrin, A. J., & Dalglish, C. (2003). *Leadership: An Australasian focus.* Milton, Australia: John Wiley.

Fournier, V., & Grey, C. (2000). At the critical moment: Conditions and prospects for critical management studies. *Human Relations, 53*(1), 7–32.

Goleman, D. (2005). *Emotional intelligence* (10th ed.). New York: Bantam.

Gronn, P. (1999). *The making of educational leaders.* London: Cassall.

Hersey, P., Blanchard, K. H., & Johnson, D. E. (1996). *Management of organizational behaviour: Utilizing human resources* (7th ed.). Upper Saddle River, NJ: Prentice Hall.

Horner, M. (1997). Leadership theory: Past, present and future. *Team Performance Management, 3*(4), 270–287.

Jackson, B., & Parry, K. (2001). *The hero manager: Learning from New Zealand's top chief executives.* Auckland, New Zealand: Penguin.

Knepfer, G. (1990). *Women of power: Playing it by their own rules.* Milson Point, Australia: Hutchinson.

Kouzes, J. M., & Posner, B. Z. (1995). *The leadership challenge: How to get extraordinary things done in organizations* (2nd ed.). San Francisco, Australia: Jossey-Bass.

Kouzes, J. M., & Posner, J. (2003). *The leadership challenge workbook.* San Francisco: Jossey-Bass.

Leavy, B. (2003). Understanding the triad of great leadership – Context, conviction and credibility. *Strategy & Leadership, 31*, 56–60.

Limerick, D., Cunnington, B., & Crowther, F. (2002). *Managing the new organisation: Collaboration and sustainability in the post-corporate world* (2nd ed.). Crows Nest, Australia: Allen & Unwin.

McGregor, D. (1960). *The human side of enterprise.* New York: McGraw-Hill.

Owens, R. G. (2004). *Organizational behaviour in education: Adaptive leadership and school reform* (8th ed.). Boston: Pearson Education.

Saal, F. E., & Knight, P. A. (1988). *Industrial organizational psychology: Science and practice.* Pacific Grove, CA: Brooks Cole.

Schein, E. H. (1985). *Organizational culture and leadership.* San Francisco: Jossey-Bass.

Shapiro, J. P., & Stefkovich, J. A. (2001). *Ethical leadership and decision making in education: Applying theoretical perspectives to complex dilemmas.* Mahwah, NJ: Lawrence Erlbaum Associates.

Stogdill, R. M. (1974). *Handbook of leadership: A survey of theory and research.* New York: Free Press.

Chapter 2

Costello, T. (1998). *Streets of hope: Finding God in St Kilda.* St Leonards, Australia: Allen & Unwin and Albatross Books.

Costello, T. (1999). *Tips from a travelling soul-searcher.* St Leonards, Australia: Allen & Unwin.

Costello, T., & Millar, R. (2000). *Wanna bet? Winners and losers in gambling's luck myth.* St Leonards, Australia: Allen & Unwin.

Costello, T. (2005). *Human Rights: The ethical underpinning of globalisation?* Focus on Rights series address given at the The Bob Hawke Prime Ministerial Centre, University of South Australia, 22 March, 2005. Retrieved February 1, 2006 from http://www.hawkecentre.unisa.edu.au/events/lectures/costello.htm

Foreword: Ten things you didn't know about ... Tim Costello, minister, World Vision CEO. (2005, November 26–27). *The Weekend Australian,* p. 10.

Skeketee, M. (2005, September 24–25). PM ups the ante on foreign aid. *The Weekend Australian,* p. 25.

Australian of the Year Award 2006 (2005). Tim Costello named Victorian Australian of the Year 2006, Media Release, 25 November, 2005. Retrieved February 2, 2006, from www.australianoftheyear.gov.au

Speakers Solutions (n.d.). Reverend Tim Costello. Speakers Solutions Integrity Speaks. Retrieved December 20, 2005, from http://www.speakersolutions.com.au/speakers/rev-tim-costello.asp?cat=9

Chapter 3

Victoria Police. (2001). *About Victoria Police.* Retrieved May 2, 2006, from http://www.police.vic.gov.au/content.asp?Document_ID=44

Nixon, C. (2002, February 13). On Leadership. Official Opening of the 2002 Williamson Community leadership program. Retrieved May 2, 2006, from http://www.leadershipvictoria.org/speeches/speech_nixon2002.htm

Monash Memo. (2003). *Police chief inspires women leaders.* Retrieved May 2, 2006, from http://www.monash.edu.au/news/monashmemo/stories/20030723/nixon.html

Nixon, C. (2003, April 20). [Wisdom interviews, with Peter Thompson]. Retrieved May 2, 2006, from http://www.abc.net.au/rn/bigidea/stories/s832657.htm.)

Saferoads Conference. (2004). Key Issues, Local Solutions Conference. Victorian Local Government Road Safety Conference, 29 April–1 May 2004, Melbourne. Retrieved May 2, 2006 from http://www.saferoadsconference.com/2004/nixon.shtml

Nixon, C. (2005, October 10). [Interview by Peter Thompson, Talking Heads, ABC Television]. Retrieved May 2, 2006, from http://www.abc.net.au/talkingheads/txt/s1475936.htm

Chapter 4

Australian of the Year Awards (2006). The Hon Justice Michael Kirby AC CMG. Retrieved March 10, 2006, from www.australianoftheyear.gov.au/pages/bio.asp?pID=244).

High Court of Australia (no date). Retrieved March 8, 2006, from www.hcourt.gov.au/kirbyj.htm

Kirby, M. (2000) *Social justice, the churches and homosexuality.* Speech given to secondary school students at the Jesuit College Preparatory School. Retrieved December 20, 2005 from http://www.critpath.org/pflag-talk/socialjustice+churches.html

Kirby, M. (2001). Community Leadership Centre, *Community groups Can Do: Leadership.* Retrieved March 9, 2006, from www.ourcommunity.com.au/leadership/leadership_article.jsp?articleId=1039)

Kirby, M. (1998a). Speech given at the University of Ulster on receiving an Honorary Degree of Doctor of Letters, University of Ulster, Belfast, Northern Ireland, Thursday 14 May, 1998. Retrieved March 21, 2006, from http://www.lawfoundation.net.au/ resources/ kirb.y/papers/19980514_ulstergrad.html

Kirby, M. (1998b). *Journeying through life with the Book of Common Prayer.* Address given at the Church of St Mary the Virgin during the Choral Eucharist, Waverley Sydney, Saturday 7 November, 1998. Retrieved March 21, 2006, from http://www.lawfoundation.net.au/resources/kirby/papers/19981107_lk.html

Kirby, M. (1994). On Leadership. Williamson Community Leadership Programme. Inaugural Williamson Community Leadership Lecture. Parliament House, Melbourne.

Resources: Justice Kirby's Papers (2003). Law & Justice Foundation of New South Wales. Retrieved October 19, 2005, from www.lawfoundation.net.au/resources/kirby/profile.html

Chapter 5

Burney, L. (2003). Inaugural Speech. Extract from NSW Legislative Assembly Hansard. Article no. 35, 6/5/2003. Retrieved November 30, 2005, from http://www.nswrecon.com/linda_burney/index.html

University of Western Sydney (2004) Linda Burney. Retrieved October 17, 2005, from http://www.uws.edu.au/about/university/governance/boardsoftrustees/board membership/lburney

Chapter 6

Australian Academy of Science Media Releases (1996). Prime Minister's reception for Professor Doherty, Nobel Laureate for medical research, Wednesday, 6 November, 1996, Members Hall, Parliament House. Retrieved December 19, 2005, from http://www.science.org.au/media/doherty2.htm

Australian Academy of Science / Science Education (1996). The Australian Academy of Science interviews Australia's latest Nobel Laureate, Professor Peter Doherty, Australian Academy of Science. Retrieved September 19, 2005, from http://www.science.org.au/scientists/doherty.htm

Doherty, P. (1997). Peter C. Doherty – Autobiography. Taken from Les Prix Nobel. The Nobel Prizes 1996, Editor Tore Frangsmyr, [Nobel Foundation], Stockholm, 1997. Retrieved July 22, 2005, from http://www.nobelprize.org/nobel_prizes/medicine/laureates/1996/doherty-autobio.htm

University of Queensland (2001). Professor Peter Doherty, Nobel Laureate, Alumni. Retrieved September 19, 2005, from http://www.alumni.uq.edu.au/index.html?page=283&pid=283&ntemplate=568

Doherty, P. (2005). *The beginner's guide to winning the Nobel Prize: A life in science.* Carlton, Australia: The Miegunyah Press.

Chapter 7

Retrieved August 7, 2003 from http://www.ovations.com.au/bios/JimSoorley.shtml

Soorley, J. (2001). Mayoral matters. *The Local Bulletin.* 7 August 2003. Retrieved August 23, 2006 from http://www.thelocalbulletin.com.au/article.asp?a_id=373

Chapter 8

Ackworth School (2005). *Ackworth School: A brief introduction.* Retrieved November 28, 2005 from http://www.ackworth.w-yorks.sch.uk/orig.html

Australian Academy of Technological Sciences and Engineering Clunies Ross Award (2005). Medical science (skin tissue engineering). Retrieved October, 20 2005 from http://www.cluniesross.org.au/index.php?sectionid=20

Australian of the Year Awards 2005 (2005). Fiona Wood AM. Retrieved July 27, 2005 from http://www.australianoftheyear.gov.au/pages/page59.asp

Bond, C. (2005). How to be a doctor, mum and national heroine. Interview with Fiona Wood, *Yorkshire Post Today*, 21 September, 2005. Retrieved October 20, 2005, from http://www.yorkshiretday.co.uk/viewarticle2.aspx?sectionid=105& articleid=1195837

Hutchen, B. (2003). Episode 9 (Fiona Wood). Interview. *George Negus Tonight*. Retrieved July 28, 2005, from http://www.abc.net.au/dimensions/dimensions_ people/Transcripts/5888102.htm

Industry Search (2005). Fiona Wood calls for greater coaction in biotech sector, News Article. Retrieved October 20, 2005, from http://www.industrysearch. com.au/news/printarticle.asp?id=17514

Laurie, V. (2003, June 21–22). The great cover-up: Fiona Wood's "spray-on skin" is revolutionising. *The Weekend Australian Magazine*, pp. 18–21, microform.

Leser, D. (2005, November). Thank God for Fiona: One day with the Australian of the year. *Women's Weekly*, pp. 54–59.

Madden, C. (2005). Burning ambition, Interview with Fiona Wood, *Science Network WA: Science News Archive*. Retrieved October 20, 2005 from http://www.sciencewa.net.au/science_archive.asp?pg+30&NID=207

Chapter 9

Clean Up Australia (2004). Ian Kiernan's story. Clean Up Australia. Retrieved January 25, 2005 from http://www.cleanup.com.au/About/ian-kiernan--s-story.html

Clean Up Australia (2005). Homepage. Retrieved June 9, 2005 from http://www.cleanup.com.au/Main.asp?RequestType=Homepage&SubRequestType =Internet&CatID=1

Top Achievers, (n.d.). Ian Kiernan: Snippets of a life. Retrieved November 18, 2004 from http://www.achievers-odds.com.au/topachiever/ikiernansnip.htm

Chapter 10

Sarina Russo Group (n.d.) About Sarina Russo. Retrieved November 9, 2006 from http://www.russo.qld.edu.au/site/SRG/AboutSarinaRusso.aspx

Russo, S. (with Gleeson, R.) (2002). *Meet me at the top!* Melbourne, Australia: Crowncontent.

Chapter 11

Clarke, S. (2005, July 23–24). Life and times: How couples divide their time. *The Courier Mail*, p. 2.

Expressions Dance Company (n.d.). Maggi Sietsma AM, Founding Artistic Director. Retrieved November 9, 2006 from http://www.expressions.org.au/ founding_artistic_director.php

www.ingramcontent.com/pod-product-compliance
Ingram Content Group Australia Pty Ltd
76 Discovery Rd, Dandenong South VIC 3175, AU
AUHW011250130325
408272AU00010B/34